T0293053

HOW TO MAKE SUSTAINABILITY IRRESISTIBLE

THE

GOOD

COMMUNICATOR

VIRGINIA CINQUEMANI

Foreword by Mike Barry

First published in Great Britain by Practical Inspiration Publishing, 2025

ISBN   9781788606189 (hardback)
        9781788606196 (paperback)
        9781788606219 (epub)
        9781788606202 (mobi)

Want to bulk-buy copies of this book for your team and colleagues? We can customize the content and co-brand *The Good Communicator* to suit your business's needs.

Please email info@practicalinspiration.com for more details.

 Practical Inspiration
Publishing

Contents

Foreword

The world's on fire. It's a proven scientific fact. If we don't put the fire out we will destroy not the Planet but rather a Society that's blossomed, for many but not all, in a rare window of climatic stability in the Earth's 4.5 billion year history.

We have the technologies – solar panels, wind turbines, batteries, etc. – to put the fire out, many of which could save us money, create better neighbourhoods, and create good jobs.

A simple, compelling premise, spelt out in just 76 words.

One that surely doesn't demand a PhD to understand; extraordinary wealth to act upon; or a Mother Theresa like willingness to put the long term needs of others before the immediacy of your own life today.

Yet... the vast majority of the eight billion people alive today are not engaged in the completeness of these words.

Many are experiencing the 'fire' – the impact of growing weather extremes on lives and livelihoods. Some see the potential of the new technologies that could pull us back from the brink. A few are taking the long-term view, acting in a precautionary way to protect things that feel distant in time and geography.

But overall, too few people, taking or calling for action. Yet to 'us' it feels so obvious, why not to 'them'?

Afterall, we 'communicate' with all eight billion of 'them' – as citizens, parents, voters, savers, consumers, neighbours, work colleagues – every day on the imperative for climate action.

Yes, we can point to very dark forces that have corrupted the world of politics, business, and global discourse to protect their wealth and power. They dissemble, obfuscate, and confuse and they do it very well. But, let's be clear, these mendacious deniers are having it easy. Winning the 'war for hearts and minds' – their tropes too easily seized as a soothing balm for inaction – 'it's always happened'; 'it's not as bad as they make out'; 'it's too late to act'; 'it'll send us back to the Stone Age'.

And the response of those who believe in the imperative for climate action are generally poor. We shout back, 'see what we see'; 'read what we read'.

We don't lack for well written reports and sharp PowerPoint presentations, we have oodles of them, but rather at an emotional human level we fail to recognize people's desire for personal respect, certainty, agency, and connection to the immediate world they live in, every day.

We should never stop researching, innovating, reporting, lobbying, and marching but let's not forget that Abraham Lincoln took just 272 words to inspire a Nation broken by Civil War in his 1863 Gettysburg Address and that Martin Luther King Jr. needed just 1,667 words to share a Dream. Words matter. The way they are delivered even more.

The Good Communicator helps us rebuild our approach to communication. It dissects clearly why we are failing to communicate the need to act on the climate crisis and then, 'walking its own talk', it engages us energetically in how individually and collectively we can transform the narrative, not just on the Big Stage but also through 100s of daily conversations.

However proficient a communicator you think you are, *The Good Communicator* will leave you a better one. We need a low carbon technology revolution but we need a communication one too.

Mike Barry, Pioneer in Sustainable Business Transformation and Leadership, and Director of Sustainable Business, Plan A at Marks & Spencer (2013–2019)

A note to the reader

It was a bright winter morning at the beginning of the Green Gorilla's[1] adventure and I was excited to run my first in-person event on how to communicate sustainability.

I started by inviting people to share what was their biggest challenge when it came to communicating the sustainability message.

A charismatic and elegant man in his thirties was the last one I'd thought would say: "I feel I cannot make an impact."

He explained further that he was a sustainability consultant with years of experience, yet he was unable to convince his clients to embrace sustainability fully. He felt he was only ticking boxes and not making much of a difference to address the real issues. The rest of the room nodded.

That was truly an "aha" moment for me. Many more people than I realized at the time were struggling to communicate and sell sustainability to their clients.

Even seemingly confident people could not shift the needle.

The complexity of the sustainability scenario

Since that morning a few years ago, things seem only to have intensified and become more complex.

---

[1] My (then) newly funded training and coaching business.

The climate is changing in front of our very eyes. (As I'm writing this, I'm wearing a t-shirt. In October. In England.) And it affects every corner of the Planet with catastrophic events manifesting themselves more and more frequently: storms, wildfires, flooding and food shortages are now a regular occurrence in Europe as well as in other parts of the world.

At the time of writing, many people who feel they cannot watch this happening without intervening are being arrested because of their pacific protests in several locations around the world. Yet, every quarter, oil and gas companies report billions of pounds/dollars in profits while people are struggling to pay their bills.

It can be incredibly frustrating to see how the situation is getting out of hand and yet there is not enough momentum to change the status quo.

Currently, in the UK where I'm based, there are no clear strategies or policies to reach the elusive Net Zero target by 2050.[2] While a few countries around the world have already reached that goal, most governments seem to struggle to keep up their commitments made at each COP[3] and, rather, tend to dilute their intermediate milestones in the name of being "realistic". It feels like trying to hit a target 10 metres away with a fun fair bow and arrow.

And Net Zero would only be the beginning to slow down the devastating impact of abusing fossil fuels for hundreds of years in the name of never-ending economic growth. Replenishing and regenerating what we have lost would be a mammoth effort and the logical next step.[4]

Add to this that we haven't worked out all the solutions yet. Science is making incredible progress every day, but today's solutions are often incompatible with the current economic system based on infinite growth.

---

[2] A legal obligation ratified in 2019.

[3] The annual United Nation Climate Change Conference of the Parties.

[4] By the way, I hate the term "sustainability". I have been a sustainability professional for two decades and this word doesn't cut it anymore. Do we really want to *sustain* the status quo? However, for simplicity's sake, throughout this book I'll use the term "sustainability" to indicate a brighter, more just future and imply newer ways to define it, like Environmental Social and Governance (ESG) as it's understood in the financial and business markets, and regeneration, the attempt to replenish what's been lost and give back to Nature more than we have taken over time.

Every solution also has complex ramifications and often implies compromises – electric vehicles (EVs) being a good example of that. Yes, they reduce air and soil pollution where they are used, but unless EVs are charged with 100% renewable energy, the problem of emissions is only shifted to another location. And what happens at the end of their batteries' usable life? What about ethical labour practices and the dubious way some components are sourced (like cobalt) to make those batteries? What about the energy-intensive processes to make the vehicles' chassis and bodywork?

It isn't always clear what to do next to embrace sustainability, especially for those who do not work in this sector, like most of our clients.

However, it's not all bad news.

I have witnessed the evolution of this issue over the last two decades, and I can see some progress.

Even just five years ago, everyone involved in a project had to be convinced that sustainability was a good idea. Sustainability professionals had to work hard to demonstrate that sustainability was going to be "the future".

Today, at least a few people within organizations are already advocates and consider sustainability an obvious choice. Bids of major infrastructure and building projects have sustainability as a key component. Sir David Attenborough's TV shows have brought planetary issues into people's living rooms: according to a 2023 survey conducted among UK residents, more than 80% has some concern about climate change.[5]

And while in some countries, such as Indonesia and the USA, a large portion of the population still believes climate change is a fad or is not man-made,[6] in others, including the UK, deniers are an endangered species and the conversation has mostly shifted from "why" sustainability has to be adopted to "what" to do and "how" to implement it.

[5] Statista (2023, October 26). Level of concern about climate change in the United Kingdom 2023. www.statista.com/statistics/426733/united-kingdom-uk-concern-about-climatechange/

[6] Buchholz, K. (2020, December 3). Where climate change deniers live. Statista Daily Data. www.statista.com/chart/19449/countries-with-biggest-share-of-climate-changedeniers/

Not long ago I delivered some BREEAM[7] awareness training sessions to a UK steel building component manufacturer. During a walkthrough of their factory, the technical manager described how this carbon-intensive company is striving to make their entire operations carbon neutral: not by simply offsetting their emissions by planting trees somewhere in another part of the world as many businesses do,[8] but by installing a massive photovoltaic system to power directly their machinery. Additionally, they are seeking Environmental Product Declaration (EPD) certification for their products to ensure all the materials are responsibly sourced and as low impact as possible, while closely watching their supply chain to ensure it follows the same principles. They see carbon-neutrality as an advantage over their competitors and a needed step to ensure the longevity of their company.

Another example that the sustainability bar is raising is that, at the beginning of 2024, the Science-Based Targets initiative (SBTi)[9] revoked Net Zero commitments from over 200 companies, including some well-known names in corporate sustainability like innocent drinks, Unilever and Proctor & Gamble. These firms either failed to meet the deadline for setting comprehensive Net Zero targets or opted out of using SBTi's criteria.

Everyday struggles

With the complexity I just attempted to describe, it's no wonder that sustainability professionals and leaders everywhere still struggle to have conversations that change their clients' and boards' minds and influence them to adopt sustainability as business as usual.

---

[7] BREEAM stands for BRE Environmental Assessment Method, and it's the UK most used assessment and certification scheme to specify and measure the sustainability performance of buildings. www.breeam.com

[8] As you'll know, offsetting is not the best way to address the climate crisis we are in. While restoring habitats and increasing biodiversity by planting new trees has its obvious advantages, what we really need to do is stop pumping CO_2 into the atmosphere in the first place. Planting trees is one of the solutions to absorb the CO_2 that is already there (CO_2 can take hundreds of years to be absorbed by the ocean, plants and soil), but the capacity of oceans and plants to take up carbon is simply not keeping pace with our emissions, so it is definitely not the silver bullet that will save the day.

[9] SBTi is a corporate climate action organization enabling companies and financial institutions globally to contribute to addressing the climate crisis. Science Based Targets Initiative (n.d.). https://sciencebasedtargets.org/

Progress in this area seems modest and too slow, and the results are for everyone to see on the news. But why are we struggling to sell sustainability to others, when it's so obvious that it's the way forward?

The difficulty you and your team face in selling sustainability to others depends on the audience you are speaking to, the context and even your mindset, which we will look at in detail later in this book. For now, let me give you some examples of different companies' leaders and their challenges with sustainability. Perhaps you can identify with one of them, or you can see your clients in them.

- Jon is the CEO of a manufacturing company that produces heavy-duty work garments. He has seen an increase in costs in production and believes it's hard enough to make a profit, let alone change his company's processes and materials to be more sustainable. The bottom line, his primary focus, seems to be at odds with sustainability.

- Naomi is the CEO of a large construction company. She and her board expect sustainability to be business as usual in all the work they carry out. However, the message doesn't necessarily trickle down to the lower levels of her organization – especially the supply chain. Some subcontractors struggle to meet or even understand her requests. They are overbooked and can't spare the time to deal with this stuff.

- Priya is the MD of a small travel agent and although she would like to, she can't see how she can adapt her company's approach to embedding sustainability in the business. She believes she doesn't have the resources and, frankly, she doesn't know where to start.

- In Luca's small sustainability team, everyone is a keen environmentalist; however, the board of directors doesn't seem to share the same sentiment. They think that having a sustainability policy and measuring carbon every year is more than enough to tick the "S" box but the sustainability team are frustrated by the lack of progress, the greenwashing their marketing department is perpetrating and the uninspiring projects they work on. Luca is left with a very discontented team to manage and a huge sense of frustration.

It would be unjust to rest all the responsibility for the failure of the climate on the shoulders of the keen technical people who have the know-how to make a difference but don't know how to communicate it effectively. In fact, many factors are playing in this very complex scenario, in which multiple failures are occurring at the same time, from top to bottom of society.

- Governments are slow to act, have short-term political interests and often are too invested in the fossil fuel industry to take a significant stance. They rely on GDP (gross domestic product) as the only measure of the wellbeing of a country.

- Large businesses don't have the agility to pivot quickly and embed sustainability in their strategies, often heavily rely on fossil fuels and are embroiled in the "infinite growth in a finite resource world" lie of the current economic system.

- Small businesses don't have the means or time to consider sustainability.

- There is a deeply ingrained belief that sustainability is always the most expensive option, which keeps the demand for sustainable, high-quality products low.

- Individuals are often the scapegoats of it all. They are made to believe that they can recycle their way out of this mess and that it's their fault. And while there is power and agency in individuals, it is becoming apparent that the other actors just mentioned have a lot more weight in how the climate crisis will play out.[10]

- Sustainability often implies long-term thinking, while organizations and humans are not predisposed to work on something difficult, the potential risks of which are unknown or which provides rewards a long time into the future. Sometimes this is described as the *Principle of Least Effort*.[11]

---

[10] Historically, 70% of global fossil fuel and cement CO_2 emissions since the Industrial Revolution can be attributed to just 78 corporate and state producing entities. Carbon Majors Database. Launch Report (2024). https://carbonmajors.org/

[11] When natural responses to a situation like a fight or flight aren't possible, dangers can't be predicted or there's no established way to respond (which is the case for sustainability), our brain triggers our behavioural inhibition system (BIS) and we stop

Who this book is for

If you have picked up this book, there is a reason. Let me guess.

- You want to have better conversations that have the power to change others' behaviours.

- You might be a sustainability leader, someone who has the opportunity to raise awareness and concerns about climate change every day with high-calibre individuals and organizations, and yet can't seem to convert those conversations into significant actions.

- Alternatively, you own a sustainability business but struggle to sell your services and are getting disheartened by the status quo.

- Perhaps you are a sustainability professional – someone who consults or designs, but struggles to engage meaningfully with your clients or top management around these themes.

You probably have conversations about sustainability that include others saying, for example, "It costs too much", "It takes too much time" or "It's not a priority". As a result, you feel a range of negative emotions, from frustration to disappointment, from anger to hopelessness, from stress to depression. This might even affect your family life, as these feelings come home with you.

You might feel exhausted and that you are wasting so much time trying to convince others to do the obvious right thing. Yet you believe it is possible to have better conversations; in fact, you believe in the transformational power of those conversations.

I'm a huge advocate for *stubborn optimism* (a term coined by Christiana Figueres, the architect of the 2015 Paris Agreement and continuous inspiration for my work). In my work supporting sustainability professionals to feel more empowered to make a difference, I believe that change is possible. Not easy, but possible.

---

acting (we "freeze") to protect us from harm. As a consequence, we prefer to carry out simple tasks that give immediate satisfaction to avoid stress or inconvenience. Kunz, E. (2014). Henri Laborit and the inhibition of action. *Dialogues in Clinical Neuroscience*, 16(1), 113–117.

It would be silly and irresponsible to say "Everything will be fine!" and leave it at that. No, stubborn optimism is more than just looking at the silver lining of situations or believing that the future will be all unicorns and rainbows. It's about putting in the work, doing everything we have the power to do, whatever our roles as individuals in this society, whatever our jobs, whatever communities we belong to, and believing that if we all pull in the right direction, we will give a chance to our children to enjoy their own lives in peace like many of us have had the fortune to do.

However, individuals, on their own, can do very little. If we want to reverse the climate crisis, and all its related issues, we need to join efforts. There is power in the mass and superior intelligence that is much more than the sum of our individual intelligence.

Imagine you want to make a scrumptious cake. You might want to use high-quality ingredients, like 70% dark chocolate, creamy oat milk and organic orange zest. But will the single ingredients, as delicious as they are, ever be more delicious than the final result? If you have done a good job, the cake will always be better than each of the ingredients. This is why this book was born.

What this book will help you with

I believe in the power of individuals and I believe in the power of communication to co-create new futures with others. If, in 1963, civil rights activist Martin Luther King Jr. hadn't had a dream and hadn't shared that dream with an audience, the American civil rights legislation would not have seen the light of day.

Not only that. It's not the conversation in itself that changes the situation, it is how two or more people align, and see things in the same way. When people get together in alignment of intent, it can be transformative and the first step towards co-creating a better future for everybody.

More creative ideas will follow, and each will contribute in a way that a single idea might never be able to.

This book will take you through the journey of crafting transformative conversations with clients, colleagues and board members to build up solid rapport, not to con people into doing something they don't want to do.

If you normally use your data as your crutch, I'll show you how leading the conversation from a place of empathy and understanding can have much more impactful results, and you can use data as a corroborating element, instead of the main tool. Statistics and percentages do not change anything unless they are part of a larger narrative tailored to your specific audience.

Yes, it will take a bit of work to structure your conversations differently from now on, but if you follow this step-by-step approach, it will soon become second nature, and you'll be able to instruct people in your team to do the same.

This approach will not only have the result of allowing your team to win more work with clients, but to strengthen your relationship with them, and to build something truly transformational. To transform the way your board of directors think about sustainability, and embed it into their strategy. To recruit more sustainability champions in your company.

As human beings, we might think that there is only one solution to a problem. But in reality, in sustainability – like in anything in life – there are potentially infinite possibilities and solutions. Changing our conversations from an exchange of technical information to a co-creation process will unlock many of these possibilities in a way that was unimaginable before.

How to use this book

You don't need to read this book cover to cover, although doing so can help you have a more transformative experience. If you believe you have already mastered some of the techniques, you can skip those and go to the parts you are interested in exploring further.

Throughout the book, you'll be able to reflect on the ideas I offer you via action and reflection points so that you can apply the learning immediately and see what works for you. (You'll find those by downloading the workbook from www.thegreengorilla.co.uk/the-good-communicator. I'm all about practicality, and this is a practical book.)

The book is split into three parts.

Part 1 is an introduction to the psychological aspects of the climate crisis and of influencing others. You may well find sustainability obvious, and because you are likely to surround yourself with other people thinking along the same lines, you might have a perception that *everyone* thinks in the same way – the so-called *confirmation bias*. However, not everyone thinks the same. Otherwise, we would not be in a crisis. The intent of this part of the book is therefore to clarify the seemingly small difference between the way sustainability professionals think and feel about sustainability versus the rest of the world: this is key to having better communication, crossing that barricade and influencing others.

Part 2 is intended to help you shift your audience mindset to communicate sustainability successfully, by understanding what your audience is thinking, and how to quickly adapt your message so that it resonates with them, no matter their opinion on the climate crisis, or their objections to the solutions you propose. If your message resonates, they will be more likely to trust you and eventually, buy into your ideas. Finally, I'm assuming you are a leader, or aspiring to be. I'll show you how you can coach your team to become influencing communicators of sustainability too.

Part 3 of the book is the Good Communicator framework, which you'll be using to structure your conversations. It's a five-step process that will take you and your audience on a journey to shift their perceptions, land on the same page and work together to co-create powerful results.

Be mindful that we learn better by doing and from real-life situations, so the more often you can use the techniques in your day-to-day conversations, the more skilled you'll become and the results will follow.

Ready?

Grab your favourite beverage, get comfy and let's get started.

Acknowledgements

It takes a village to raise a child and, as I had the opportunity to discover over the last year, it takes a nurturing community of supportive, like-minded individuals to write a book.

The Good Communicator is the product of thousands of conversations with brilliant sustainability practitioners frustrated by the lack of progress towards a better future, as well as seemingly unpersuadable people, over my career as a sustainability professional, trainer and coach; many hours of coaching practice with amazing coaching clients who want to make a difference to this planet; my Stakeholder Engagement and Communication lessons when I was teaching them at Coventry University, UK.

In particular, though, I'd like to thank a few key people to whom I owe a great deal:

- My family, first and foremost, for putting up with me, my long hours at my desk and the not-so-nutritional meals they had to endure while I was working full steam on making this book the best it could be.

- My coaching clients, who probably don't know it but who provide an infinite source of inspiration to me as a sustainability professional and human being; in particular, "Carmen", who ignited the initial spark that led me to write this book – please, keep on doing the amazing work you do; you got this.

- My generous and brilliant peer reviewers: Carrie, Ben and Amit, who provided so much useful feedback, ideas and encouragement, and gave their precious time to read the first appalling version of the manuscript.

- All the invincible sustainability professionals who kindly agreed to share their experiences with me to be featured in this book – you have truly given colour and depth to my words.

- Alison Jones and her marvellous team at Practical Inspiration Publishing for believing in my ideas and supporting me throughout this journey – I'm forever grateful for this opportunity.

- You, my dear reader, for trusting in my words and having the courage to work on yourself, and start this process of growth and improvement in the name of the common, greater good.

And finally, I'd like to thank myself for believing in me and never, ever giving up. Writing this book has been one of the hardest things I've ever done so well done, me!

Part 1
Why is it so difficult to get others to buy into sustainability?

Figure 1

The reasons why sustainability is not mainstream yet

It's hard to interpret the current situation objectively. Especially as a sustainability professional who has worked in this industry for close to 20 years, I find it hard not to be biased: I have been surrounding myself with people who share my core beliefs and values.

My LinkedIn feed shows a homogenous stream of sustainability stories, some great, some critical of the current political climate. Still, sustainability – and its cousins Environmental, Social and Governance (ESG) and regeneration – is the word, left, right and centre.

However, I know that this is not a neutral view of the situation. So, let's try and make sense of the current situation as objectively as possible, with the disclaimer that nothing in sustainability is simple or straightforward.

1. Commitments to sustainability have grown stronger over the years… but not quite enough

Banking and insurance companies increasingly incorporate ESG considerations into risk management processes, product design, purpose statements and long-term strategies. The deadly disasters witnessed everywhere in the world from wildfires to floods, and consequent disruptions and losses, have finally made the penny drop.

Every year at the Climate Change Conferences of the Parties (COP), countries commit to increasingly stringent targets to curb emissions, mitigate the consequences of climate change, adapt to it and protect biodiversity.

Most large companies have some form of sustainability strategy and goals, with the ultimate Holy Grail: reaching Net Zero at some point in the next 25 years. Companies are also under pressure to disclose their emissions, climate-related financial information and other impacts via various schemes, in some countries obligatory, in others voluntary.[12]

Research from Sage and the International Chamber of Commerce (2022) highlighted that 90% of SMEs are eager to address climate change.[13]

So, sustainability is now mainstream? Not quite.

2. Our economic system is still based on the myth of infinite growth

"We are on a highway to climate hell with our foot on the accelerator," the UN Secretary-General António Gutierrez told world leaders at the opening of the COP27 held in Egypt in 2022. The window of opportunity to avoid climate disaster is narrowing rapidly and the exponential growth of carbon emissions in the atmosphere (with a tiny inflection during the COVID pandemic in 2020) demonstrates that he's right. In 1850, the world emitted 197 million tonnes of carbon dioxide. In 2021 it emitted 188 times more (37 billion tonnes), without any sign of change of this trajectory in the future.

---

[12] In 2022, the UK was the first G20 country to impose Climate-Related Financial Disclosure to publicly quoted companies, large private companies and LLPs in line with Task Force on Climate-Related Financial Disclosures (TCFD) recommendations. Department for Energy Security and Net Zero (2022, February 21). Climate-related financial disclosures for companies and limited liability partnerships (LLPs). GOV. UK.www.gov.uk/government/publications/climate-related-financial-disclosures-for-companies-and-limited-liability-partnerships-llps
[13] Sage (2023). *Path for Growth: Making sustainability reporting work for SMEs.* In www.sage.com/en-gb/company/sustainability-and-society/planet/

Governments are not taking quick enough action – and in some cases, they are slowing it down. The reasons are many, but they can all be combined into one: the current economic system. The current economic system focuses on GDP and the infinite growth of this number as the main measure of the financial health of a country. Trouble is, this measure is a myth. It doesn't take into consideration the social wellbeing of a country, it doesn't tell us how prosperity is shared out in society, and it is connected to higher carbon emissions – which, as we have all been witnessing in recent years, carry devastating societal and environmental consequences. GDP also encourages the exploitation of countries in the Global South.

Finally, and most importantly, how can the economy grow endlessly on a Planet with finite resources? Sustainable development and "thriving within the planetary boundaries", as suggested by Kate Raworth's *Doughnut Economics*,[14] model seems a utopia.

Sustainability is mostly a tick-box exercise without substantial actions to back up the commitments because it is still perceived as expensive and too long-term. It's easier and quicker (and incredibly short-sighted) to drill more oil in the North Sea. Of course, we cannot wean ourselves off oil and gas overnight. That would be suicidal and unrealistic. But, eventually, to avoid climate hell, renewable energy will need to be the main power source. A circular economy will need to substitute almost entirely the current linear *make-use-discard* paradigm. Regeneration will need to happen in a coordinated and strategic way to salvage and replenish lost resources and to absorb the excess of CO_2 in the atmosphere. Societal and environmental wellbeing will need to be the main measure a country uses to track progress.

But political cycles are too short to do that. Politicians in charge can't demonstrate meaningful results within the short space of their mandates. So, they don't embrace sustainable change because they can't see what's in it for them.

---

[14] Raworth, K. (2018). *Doughnut Economics: Seven Ways to Think Like a 21st-Century Economist.*

3. Sustainability is a slippery fish

A few years ago, I bought a bamboo coffee cup from a local zero-waste shop. So pretty, with its pink and brown flowery retro design. Is there anything in the world that screams "I'm a tree hugger" more than a reusable coffee cup? And with my obvious addiction to caffeine, this was the perfect solution... Until news came that bamboo coffee cups (and other tableware, including baby plates and cups) contain melamine and formaldehyde, which get released in contact with hot liquid, posing a serious health threat to users.

The science of sustainability is forever evolving.

There are new discoveries about what is sustainable and what isn't on a regular basis – which is obviously a good thing, but it also makes our work as sustainability professionals incredibly difficult. We can rarely reassure our clients that a certain solution will be the most sustainable one forever. Often not building or not buying new are the most sustainable solutions. Other times, you have to because the current solution is wasteful and might even pose a health risk to people and the Planet – e.g. an existing industrial system that doesn't filter waste before discharging it into local watercourses, or school buildings containing reinforced autoclaved aerated concrete (RAAC).

The prevailing consensus by scientists is that fossil fuels are the main contributor to climate change; renewable energy sources are the alternative but other sustainability solutions cannot offer the same reassurance that they will be the best solution forever. Not having certainty over sustainable solutions might be one of the reasons why they haven't become mainstream yet. People prefer to stick to what they know instead of taking the leap into the unknown.

4. People do not respond to long-term threats and opportunities

While I believe the baton stops at the governments and companies responsible for 70% of our global emissions, the human psyche has a role to play in all of this. After all, governments are led by people and so are the big oil companies.

Daniel Gilbert, a Professor of Psychology at Harvard (USA), argues that our brain is essentially a "get-out-of-the-way machine".[15] We are wired to respond rapidly and decisively to immediate threats. Remember the global response to COVID-19? Almost overnight new rules, policies, protective equipment and behaviours were created to protect us from a scary sudden threat.

What about long-term threats? We are not wired to see danger when it comes gradually. We are used to adaptation. The history of our evolution is a brilliant demonstration of this unique capacity to change as a response to our environment. Of course, we have relatively recently learned to save up towards our pensions and to look after our bodies to prevent future illness. But even those signs of "long-termism" are not traits that all human beings share. Otherwise, there would be no credit card debts or obesity.

Some researchers hypothesize that we are also very accustomed to responding quickly to other human beings' actions (say, terrorism) and other visually-evoked threats, but climate change doesn't have a face.[16] As for the COVID-19 virus, even my then five-year-old could draw it clearly and understand what it meant. The threat from climate change is not an identifiable villain we can demonize so easily.

5. People do not act unless the threat is personal

One summer a few years ago I travelled back to Sicily to visit my family. One morning, as I was walking towards the newsagent to buy a newspaper, I saw an old man opening the door of his car and dumping the contents of his vehicle onto the street: a plastic bottle, some old receipts, pistachio shells, a biro pen. I can still remember how the blood in my whole body rushed to my head in three seconds flat.

I was so furious, I stomped towards his car and started shouting at him (note: this is NOT the way I suggest you communicate sustainability

---

[15] Harvard Thinks Big 2010 – Daniel Gilbert – "Global Warming and Psychology" [Video] (2010, March 21). Vimeo. https://vimeo.com/10324258
[16] Balban, M. Y. et al. (2021). Human responses to visually evoked threat. *Current Biology*, 31(3), 601–612, e3.

to others but stay with me here): "What are you doing?! Why are you dumping your rubbish on the street?!"

He shouted back – of course, he did. "Who are you?! And why do you care? I pay my council tax and the street cleaners will take care of it. That's what they are there for."

Such a moronic and exploitative answer inflamed me even more: "Do you treat your home like this?? Dumping crap on the floor?"

He said, "My house is spotless, you… !" – and then he used an expletive I cannot share here but you can imagine what that was.

Many people just don't care about anything that is happening outside their homes or themselves. If it's not personal, someone else will take care of it. Arguably, we all just care about what's in it for us. For some of us, that means the environment because we love it, and we feel a connection to it. But over the centuries, our collective connection with the environment has weakened to become less of a co-creative partnership and more of a systematic exploitation campaign. The environment is seen by many as something to use for their own return, that exists only to maintain their lifestyles.

We have forgotten that our astonishing complex and interconnected Planet has unique "Goldilocks" conditions that allow it to thrive. We have forgotten that we are, in fact, just a blip in the millions of years of existence of the universe. In fact, if the universe's life were as long as a marathon, we would have been around for half a step. We have evolved to thrive in challenging conditions by learning from our ancestors how to exploit the Planet.

Ever since developing more of our calculating, egotistic left-brain hemisphere, we have started seeing ourselves as detached from the rest. What's more, we act as if we are the only species worth living (except some cute ones we think we can take along on our journey, like Pomeranian dogs). We cannot even imagine ever facing the dodos' and dinosaurs' fate.

But we forget that we are interconnected with every element on this Planet and that our species can only survive as part of the fragile, complex and perfectly balanced system we rely on.

6. Convenience

Friday evenings in the UK is traditionally seen by some as fish and chips night. Imagine, for example, you have worked hard all day, then cooked dinner every evening of the week, and you want to just slump on the sofa and watch TV. You order via your favourite delivery company's app. Your food will be with you by the time you have chosen a movie and changed into your loungewear.

Convenient. Easy. You don't even have to walk to the fish and chip shop anymore.

Absolutely nothing wrong with a takeaway now and then – I'm not getting into an argument about takeaway boxes, food miles and sustainable fishing here. This is just a little example of how we often prefer convenience (remember the *Principle of Least Effort*?) to doing work that might result in healthier or more sustainable choices.

We live in a culture of convenience: food, clothes, transportation and so on. The issue is that sustainable choices are still, in many cases, more expensive, less flashy and harder work than their alternatives, e.g.:

- disposable plastic vs. refillable containers

- cheap sweat-shop clothes vs. second-hand or high-end sustainable brands

- fast food vs. home-cooked and organic

- jumping in the car vs. taking the bus or cycling

- buy-now-with-a-click from an e-commerce giant vs. walking to independent shops.

Sustainability will be mainstream only when it becomes more convenient and cheaper than its unsustainable alternatives.

7. Discourses of climate delay

So, what do we do as a consequence of all of the things we have so far discussed?

We delay. We pass on responsibility to others. We deal with perceived bigger threats (more urgent as they will have short-term consequences, not necessarily more important).

You might have come across a range of "discourses of climate delay",[17] which accept the existence of climate change but justify inaction or limited efforts. Here are some examples of these mindsets and how they show up in conversations.

- **Disruptive change is not necessary.**
  - "Technology will save us, one day."
  - "All we need to do it to declare a climate emergency and set some targets" "Fossil fuels are part of the solution: they are becoming more efficient."
  - "Let's opt for voluntary action."

- **It's not possible to mitigate climate change.**
  - "We cannot combine reducing emissions with our current lifestyle, therefore we won't do anything."
  - "Too little too late, we should therefore adapt."

- **Someone else should take action first.**
  - "Individuals are responsible for taking action to address climate change."[18]
  - "Why should we reduce emissions when China is freely pumping CO_2 in the atmosphere?"

- **Change will be too disruptive.**
  - "Fossil fuels are required for development. We would put poorer people into hardship if we switch to renewables."
  - "Climate actions will be expensive and vulnerable members of society will bear the costs."

- **We either do it perfectly or don't do it at all.**
  - "We should seek only perfect solutions everyone must buy into."

---

[17] Lamb, W., Mattioli, G., Levi, S., Roberts, J., Capstick, S., Creutzig, F., and Steinberger, J. (2020). Discourses of climate delay. *Global Sustainability*, 3, E17. doi: 10.1017/sus.2020.13
[18] This is a deflection campaign initiated by big corporations as far back as the 1980s – inspired by the gun, tobacco and beverage companies – for whom it's business as usual while they cause most of the damage and push unsustainable solutions to consumers. Mann, E. M. (2021). *The New Climate War*.

While climate change deniers still exist despite scientific evidence (5% of Americans, around 17 million individuals, think the climate is not changing and another 15% think that it is changing but not because of human activities)[19], many people among those who do believe in climate change have chosen to argue against rapid action – which is causing stalling. What's worse, many people in power hold these beliefs. It's much easier to say: "Others need to start first" and get on with our lives than keep fighting a faceless threat, which we don't know exactly when and how it will hit us. It's a sort of Russian roulette we are playing, in the name of self-preservation.

Add to this that human beings generally hate uncertainty. Not knowing what's going to happen is deeply destabilizing. So, we desperately seek some certainty, even if negative, such as "We are doomed".

What's more disconcerting is that this way of thinking has sneaked into the conscience of some environmentalists too. Bombarded with increasingly bad news of climate disasters and their consequences, they have chosen to believe that we are doomed, and so rapid action is useless.

I came across this not long ago, when I attended a local Fixers event, during which some generous handy people repair appliances and bikes for free. While I was waiting for my old bread machine to be looked at, I had a conversation with a woman I've known for years, a very active volunteer at our local sustainability charity. She shared with me that she believes we cannot do anything anymore to save the Planet and, therefore, she has chosen to support local community initiatives that help to adapt rather than "wasting time" with global ones.

Her argument did make me think. I admire her efforts at the local level. Acting locally means we have more connection with the actions and their direct positive impacts on others and the environment, which are usually immediately visible (like cleaning rivers and fixing old appliances). Those "others" are friends, family and neighbours. They have *faces*. All of this contributes to providing a strong motivation to act.

[19] Buchholz, K. (2020, December 3). *Where climate change deniers live*. Statista Daily Data. www.statista.com/chart/19449/countries-with-biggest-share-of-climate-changedeniers/

Then I thought about her initial strong assumption that we are doomed to a future of hellish freak weather, food shortages and civil unrest, which is not what the scientific community currently says. Admittedly, it doesn't look good, but scientists say we still have a few years before we hit major irreversible climate tipping points. And we have managed in the past to turn massive global problems on their heads quite quickly, like the well-known ozone hole issue.

In the late 1970s and early 1980s, scientists observed the ozone layer thinning over Antarctica's Halley Bay. They linked it to chlorofluorocarbons (CFCs) from aerosols and cooling devices, triggering global concern over serious health and ecosystem risks. This news led to unprecedented global collaboration among governments. For the first time, the urgency of the situation galvanized the world to work together to address a global environmental threat. The 1987 Montreal Protocol phased out harmful chemicals, leading to significant ozone layer recovery. By 2009, 98% of those chemicals were phased out. Today, the ozone layer is on a path to recovery and no longer constitutes a threat.

Although on that occasion there were fewer vested interests in CFCs than there are today in fossil fuels, this demonstrates that rapid, global and decisive action is possible *if we pull together.*

I concluded that doomism is not for me – yet. Not until reputable scientists tell me that I should throw in the towel and retreat as a fine artist in the Alps. If you are with me on this, we need to do something, and pretty quickly, to avoid the aforementioned climate hell.

The "equilibrist challenge": striking the right tone in climate communication

Sandra S is an event organizer and workshop facilitator.

With a strong communication background, I believe I can have a big impact by raising awareness around climate change, the Sustainable Development Goals and the reasons for action from the first interactions I have with clients: the first step to change is awareness.

However, the emphasis I give to those facts through the stories I tell had to change over time.

Now it is more motivational and positive, focusing on what we can still do without ignoring the seriousness of our situation.

Striving for this "right" balance like an equilibrist is the challenge I have put on myself, but I can confidently say that the way you tell the story determines how many people you recruit to the sustainability cause and their level of engagement.

From communication to co-creation: the key to a sustainable future

My thoughts around the solutions have evolved over time but the importance of communication to change the status quo has been central in my work at Green Gorilla since Day One. Having had the opportunity to speak to thousands of sustainability professionals over the years via my work as a trainer in previous roles, I realized that it isn't technical prowess that sustainability professionals, and especially leaders, need.

There are plenty of higher education degrees, professional certifications and qualifications that can make you into a technical wizard. And you probably have accumulated quite a few of those over the years. Moreover, major institutions and membership organizations offer plenty of opportunities to upskill in all aspects of sustainability – and we need those because sustainability is a fluid and ever-changing science.

But what they don't offer *en masse* is communication training. As communication can stand in the way of effective action, it is of paramount importance that sustainability professionals hone this skill.

Our inability to communicate sustainability to others

It may be difficult to accept, but we need to eat a little humble pie and admit that as a species we have forgotten (did we ever know how?!) how to communicate with others meaningfully.

I'm trying not to sound like my lovely great-auntie who didn't know how to write and thought the Italian prime minister was the Pope, but technology has been a double-edged sword in our quest for faster communication. In fact, technology has hindered our ability to connect with others at a deep level as we increasingly hide behind a screen instead of talking to people face to face.

As a rational and probably highly educated person, who has sustainability as a core value, you might believe that logic and data are your power tools to convince others that sustainability is the obvious solution to every issue. In the research phase of this book, I asked several sustainability professionals at different levels of seniority about their approach to communicating sustainability. These are some of their stories.

Sara is a circular economy consultant for a public authority.

Sara struggles to communicate the benefits of circularity to colleagues who fear losing their jobs in the waste department if those principles, aimed at reducing waste, are fully implemented. They come up with counter-arguments that she doesn't feel equipped to answer, so she feels stuck. Her communication strategy is based on pushing the local authority's Net Zero and circular economy strategies.

Ruxandra is an experienced architect with a passion for sustainability.

Years ago, Ruxandra pivoted her practice to focus on sustainable design and now tries to work mainly with clients that share her same values. However, she admits that she hasn't found a way to sell sustainability to clients who only focus on profit – which, in her experience of working on small projects, are the majority. She assumes that a change of mindset is very unlikely. When I asked her what she would change if she had a magic wand, she answered: "I wish I had the tools and time to gather evidence related to the financial benefits of sustainability."

Mark[20] is a senior project manager who focuses on sustainability for a public authority.

Mark also struggles to quantify benefits, especially for his colleagues in the finance department. However, through his efforts to demonstrate to them that long term it would cost a lot more not to adopt sustainability, he's realized that economic impacts cannot always make the case alone.

What do these three brilliant, qualified, experienced sustainability professionals have in common? They believe facts and data alone will persuade people that sustainability is the right way to go.

Why doesn't this approach work? Facts and data are important (they constitute the evidence to justify investments), but to shift the needle and get people to sign on the dotted line for an investment, they need to be integrated within a wider communication strategy that aims at grabbing the attention of the audience with emotions and meaning. This is the first necessary step towards influencing others to embrace your ideas. If what you say sounds boring or irrelevant to them, or even a threat to their current status quo, you have no hope they'll buy into your ideas. Neuroscience has demonstrated that attention and memory are aroused by anything that directly affects us as human beings[21] – we need to feel *personally* involved and emotionally touched by something

---

[20] Not his real name.
[21] Medina, J. (2008). *Brain Rules: 12 Principles for Surviving and Thriving at Work, Home and School.*

to become interested in it. We need to understand why we should pay attention to it and "what's in it for us", not just as a company but as individuals, before we seek all the details to seal the deal. And that's where you probably need to do a little more homework before entering your next important meeting.

Tailored approaches to board engagement: addressing varying levels of sustainability awareness

Sandra S, the event organizer and workshop facilitator we met earlier.

The most common challenge I face is when a board management team is not engaged towards Net Zero or they don't understand the urgency for their company to act. In my line of work the problem is less climate scepticism, as this has decreased over time, but much more being accountable on a personal and company level. Many still think they cannot change anything and this is where we need to focus our communication efforts – everyone can make a difference.

When engaging with my audiences, I use different strategies depending on their role within the company and level of "maturity" towards sustainability. For this reason, I spend considerable time understanding and getting to know my audience. Some require an "impact" presentation where the facts are presented as they are. With board members my aim is to spark a wake up call: as leaders, it is their responsibility to act (or they and their company will fail spectacularly). Otherwise, running an awareness programme requiring collaboration and collective intelligence (like Climate Fresk or Climate Pitch) helps embark a majority of employees from all levels in the transformation process of the company as it gives them a degree of agency over it.

Putting our boxing gloves on

Communication is a so-called "soft skill". But the reality is that there is nothing "soft" in trying to communicate sustainability. If anything, sometimes it feels like a fight you have to train for. In fact, this is what prompted me to write this book.

In the spring of 2023, I was having a coaching conversation with a client in a London café. Carmen,[22] a sustainability professional with more than 15 years of experience, wanted to overcome her biggest challenge, her inability to influence others to adopt sustainability. When I asked her about the last time she managed to influence someone with her ideas, she replied that it was probably a few years beforehand. As surprising as it sounds for someone who has the opportunity to talk about sustainability every single day, her challenge is not uncommon in this industry.

To explore this further I asked her what her "recipe" was for a conversation in which she felt that she had positively influenced the other person. She thought for a moment, then she said that one ingredient was not letting her passion overcome her, which would make her look unprofessional or overly emotional. The second ingredient would have been to prepare thoroughly for the fight, step into the ring and put her boxing gloves on. As she was saying that, she stopped mid-sentence then exclaimed: "Wait, why am I using all this fighting language?!"

She was bewildered at her own choice of words. She continued: "Life is already hard. How can I find the energy to prepare for a fight every day when there are so many other things to do?"

She hit the nail on the head. We often feel like the soldiers in the environmental and social justice army. Even our language is aggressive: *tackling the climate crisis, fighting climate change…*

Because sustainability is, for most of us, a lifestyle as well as a core value, we are more invested in it than if it was just a job to pay the bills. Additionally, we have families, friends, pets and the like to attend to. As leaders, we have to take care of our teams. There is not much energy

---

[22] Not her real name.

left at the end of the day to "tackle" or "fight". We tell ourselves that we are doing what we can but deep down we are frustrated because our efforts don't necessarily translate into tangible results.

So, what can we do?

Learning how to communicate to co-create

When Carmen shared her challenges in influencing others during that coaching session, I could see her energies being sapped by the thought of preparing to fight before a conversation. So, I asked her when she had felt the most *energized* in a conversation.

She thought for a moment, then replied it was when she built the conversation together with the other person, each adding a bit so that the sum of the parts is better than the individual elements. And, if she found she had something in common with the other person, the conversation wouldn't be about what she thought or wanting to convince the other person anymore, it would become a quest to get to know them better. It would be about using the common ground to build that conversation.

Carmen looked relieved as if a 20-ton boulder had just been lifted from her shoulders. She had realized that in a fight we are enemies.

Right now, all human beings are in a global crisis together, whether they know and accept it or not. We have already experienced shortages of natural materials and food caused by the unpredictable weather patterns in all four corners of the globe. We *have* common ground with others: highlighting that, and how it is affecting their businesses and everyday lives, will build that conversation and, in turn, the rapport with them. The result of this will be to find common solutions to our diverse issues and goals. To co-create new futures together with our clients and audiences, not to fight them in the name of our ideals. And when we approach a conversation as our most authentic selves, instead of as this goofy pretend knight with no armour or experience, we will feel more energized, harness our collective creativity and knowledge, and have much better, long-lasting results.

The psychology of influencing: the predictably irrational way humans behave

L ooking back at the last paragraphs of the previous chapter, you could easily argue that this all sounds really wonderful, but it's so far from your reality that you think it is impossible. Your clients/top management/colleagues (pick and choose your daily struggle here) are as hard to crack as a hazelnut when you only have your bare hands. Layers and layers of strong, ingrained beliefs prevent them from seeing your point of view, and the usual excuses pop up at every meeting, e.g.:

- "We don't have the resources."

- "We are short-staffed."

- "It's too expensive."

- "It would be nice to have but we have other priorities at the moment."

Ben, the Head of Sustainability of a large manufacturing company, told me that when his team tried to convince top management to make sustainability integral to their company's strategy, it felt like they were all outside an impenetrable castle throwing arrows and stones but unable to crack even the smallest breach open.

And that's a common reality most environmental and sustainability professionals have been facing for many years. A few years ago, trying to find a solution to this problem, my mind went to those professionals who have to influence others for a living, where the "others" are not business people, but rather desperate people who threaten to kill innocent bystanders if their conditions are not met.

Meet the hostage negotiators. Special agents trained to deal with death or life situations manage to get armed people with nothing to lose to give up hostages and turn themselves in to the authorities. Sometimes it doesn't go that smoothly, and lives are lost. Often though, hostage negotiators manage to save the hostages unharmed and catch the perpetrators dead or alive.

How could it be that technically trained and articulate professionals can't convince their rational clients or bosses to adopt sustainability, but hostage negotiators can get armed lunatics to come out of their hiding spots with their hands up? What did these people know that my fellow sustainability champions don't?

Having studied the recollections of some of the most successful FBI (the US Federal Bureau of Investigation) hostage negotiators, I've intertwined some of their techniques to influence others and to better understand human psychology when it comes to behavioural change in the next pages.

Let's open the door of the castle

Remember my client who realized she was using fighting language when referring to her work as a sustainability professional? We fight and try to shove sustainability down our clients' and board members' throats (delightful image, I know). It may feel like pushing a boulder uphill, and we wonder why we are so exhausted and frustrated all the time and don't have anything to show for our efforts! We feel *they* are the problem because they don't understand an obvious truth.

Here is an idea: *What if, instead of pushing the boulder uphill, we removed the boulder altogether? What if, instead of trying to get inside the castle by throwing stones at it, we ask how we can open that door?* Influencing others is all about removing the barriers.

Human beings are irrational

Let's start with the fact that human beings are deeply irrational. Yes, even those of us with impressive-sounding degrees and written publications under our belts. We think we follow logic and principles, but when it comes to making a decision, emotions sway us. We often make decisions based on past experiences and social norms rather than logic. Even money is not always the main driver. We care more about what others think than what we really need or can afford to have. Let me give you a personal example.

In 2021 I got a job as a university lecturer nearly 100 miles away from where I live. At the time, I had been driving a faithful Ford vehicle for many years. A workhorse that never let me down. But a petrol workhorse all the same.

Teaching environmental management while driving that car back and forth up the motorway was a contradiction. I calculated that I was going through approximately 42kg of CO_2 every time I drove there. That's more than half my body weight. So, I had a big ethos-based reason for switching to an electric vehicle. That said, I can honestly say I eventually switched because I was worried my colleagues and students would label me a hypocrite. I made a mostly emotional purchase based on social norms and justified it retrospectively with logic.

You'd think big decision-makers in companies you deal with do it differently.

But very often emotions are present in the boardroom more than you'd think and people are more likely to change if they perceive that others are changing too.

Social pressure works whether you are a teenager or a middle-aged man. Knowing this can help you deal with your next pitch to a client in a more sophisticated way.

As we will come to learn, influencing others and communicating sustainability in a way that changes people's behaviour implies honing some key skills such as tactical empathy and active listening, which will allow you to deal with different people and situations in an effective way.

The SCARF model of social behaviour applied to business interactions

Even though we are all different, as human beings we tend to be triggered by similar stimuli when it comes to communication. In 2008, neuroscientist David Rock formulated[23] five "social domains" that influence our behaviour in social situations: **status, certainty, autonomy, relatedness and fairness**. These activate in our brain the same "threat and reward" instinctive responses we rely on for physical survival (like if we were running away from a hungry bear), which we find very difficult to control.

Knowing these five domains can help you to avoid the triggers of a "threat" response from your audience and activate the "reward" mechanism that releases dopamine in their brains instead.

Status

This is our perceived relative importance to others. If, for instance, you have been hired to advise your client, beware of imposing your views: your client might feel their status and authority is under attack. A better way forward is to come across as a partner ready to help them. This will also establish the perfect conditions for co-creation, as we will explore further in this book.

A key question to ask yourself in conversations is: *Am I portraying myself as a partner ready to help, so that my audience don't feel their current or future status is under threat?*

---

[23] Rock, D. (2008). *SCARF: A Brain-Based Model for Collaborating With and Influencing Others.*

Certainty

This is our ability to predict the future, which in sustainability is usually non-existent. Because of the fluidity and ever-changing nature of this subject, we don't have much certainty about what's going to happen to the Planet or our species. In projects, some of the technologies we are using currently deemed as sustainable might not be such in the future, and in many sectors, there is little to no track record of solid results from sustainable approaches.

No wonder some clients and board directors don't want to be pioneers and don't trust the innovations you might suggest. At times, your audience might not know enough about the technologies and research behind them. Even so, you can still present relevant case studies to demonstrate at least some of the advantages of these technologies and approaches. This can provide some reassurance that they are not so experimental after all. Or perhaps you'll need to explain how a certain technology works in simple terms or a process step by step.

Key questions to ask yourself in conversations are: *Have I explained the project in enough detail? Are all the project's expectations, milestones, processes and outcomes clear?*

Autonomy

Our sense of control over events is important to all of us. When a company goes through change, individual autonomy is usually lost in the process. People are forced to adopt new ways of working and work with people they never have before. Losing one's autonomy is not a pleasant experience. We all like to feel in charge of our little patch and hate the imposition of something new, especially if this hasn't been explained to us properly or if we haven't been involved in the decision-making process.

It's important therefore to be completely transparent about what's involved in embracing sustainability and giving people some form of choice over the events.

I often make the example of giving my children the choice between vanilla and strawberry ice-cream. I'm fine with both but they feel empowered to choose the flavour they prefer between the two – note, the choice does not involve chocolate. Translating this into your work, make sure you always offer a couple of sustainable options to choose from, where you will be fine with either option.

A key question to ask yourself in conversations is: *Have I done enough to ensure my audience retains some control and agency over the project?*

Relatedness

This has to do with how safe we feel with others. Building rapport is absolutely fundamental to establishing a fruitful working relationship and co-creating truly sustainable results. Even if you (and your team) are external to the company you are supporting, you have to do the legwork to ensure you are perceived as belonging to the team, and at the very least, to be a trustworthy partner.

Small talk, which we are less and less used to because of digital communication, is actually an important part of establishing human relationships. Launching straight into working mode without having greeted one another or exchanged a minimum of pleasantries is a *faux pas* that will negatively affect your relationship with your audience. When you are holding online meetings, ask everyone to turn on their cameras. Talking to a "faceless black sea" is off-putting for the person who is speaking and makes rapport-building virtually impossible. Consider holding your meetings face-to-face whenever possible, especially the first time you meet someone new. There is no substitute for in presence relationship building.

Key questions to ask yourself in conversations are: *Have I done my best to establish a human connection with my audience? Am I coming across as transparent, trustworthy and personable?*

Fairness

If we think a new situation is not fair, we won't accept it easily. When talking about fairness, I can just picture my children when they were little, stomping their tiny feet on the floor and shouting: "It's not

FAIR!" It's very instinctive to want to be treated fairly and have the same share as others.

In sustainability, the issue of fairness translates into perceived value. If your clients or board members don't feel they have a fair deal when it comes to adopting the ideas you and your team are suggesting, they will stomp their big feet or simply say "no".

Research shows that for something to be perceived as a good deal, it has to be at least twice as good as the current solution[24] because we are all affected by biases that fight logic – in particular, *loss aversion* (we respond more strongly to losses than to gains) and *endowment bias* (if something is ours, we value it more than if it isn't). So, if something is marginally better or equal to what we already have, we don't feel it's worth the effort of switching to something different. That's where showing your audience practical examples of the numerous advantages of adopting a sustainable approach can pay off, like return on investment, protection from risks and reputation damage, talent and customer retention, and acquisition.[25] Talking just about the ethical side of sustainability will not help in most cases.

Key questions to ask yourself in conversations are: *What's in it for my audience? Have I given them enough details so that it is clear it is a fair deal for them?*

---

[24] Kahneman, D. (2015). *Thinking Fast and Slow.*
[25] Appendix C provides a list of value-created advantages of sustainability beyond the ethical argument.

Part 2
How to shift mindsets to communicate sustainability successfully

In Part 1 we have talked about some of the psychological and evolutionary reasons for why it is so difficult to get others to buy into sustainability. In this part of the book, we will use this knowledge as a starting point to shift mindsets to communicate sustainability successfully, in meetings and presentations, including if we are not natural communicators.

We will also look at how to coach your team to do the same.

The what, where, why, when, who and how of communicating sustainability

Figure 2 *Effective communication doesn't mean just conveying a message... there are many other factors to consider*

A famous quote often attributed to playwright George Bernard Shaw reads:

> The single biggest problem in communication is the illusion that it has taken place.

We commonly think of communication as speaking *to* someone or conveying a message *from* A to B. But that's a reductive way of thinking about it and, actually, the simple fact that we convey a message to others doesn't mean it is well communicated, that it has been received or that, crucially, they are going to act on it.

Communication is a complex dance of two or more dancers in which you have to know your own steps and the rules of the dance you are in, as well as anticipating the steps of other people. You have to understand whether the space you are in is suitable for the kind of dance you want to have. You have to be flexible and react according to other people's behaviour. What's more, you need to be in the right frame of mind and ensure as much as possible that others are too.

If we get into an important conversation with the wrong mindset, without having established the rules, roles and steps or having studied the other people involved beforehand, it would be like stepping on the stage of a full *Opera de Paris* to perform Tchaikowsky's *Swan Lake* without having ever rehearsed before.

Where are we going wrong?

Let's take a look at a couple of people I met a few years ago.

Georgina, an author and passionate sustainability advocate, was struggling to keep quiet among other town folks at her Parish Council's monthly public meeting.[26] That particular day, they were discussing how to address traffic congestion in the town centre and related air pollution issues. Weekend road closures and a new multi-storey car park were the two proposed solutions most people agreed on. After a few minutes of boiling inside, Georgina jumped to her feet and accused the Parish Council of being blind to climate change issues. The world is becoming an unliveable furnace, and they were not even contemplating the electrification of public transport and other low-carbon solutions like electric bike share schemes. "What a load of muppets!" she thought – and almost said.

---

[26] A parish council is a civil local authority in England and the lowest tier of local government.

Georgina felt flustered. Her hands were flapping above her head while she tried to make her point to a load of straight and mostly scornful Councillor faces. Needless to say, her outburst was quickly dismissed by the Chairman, who said that although her concerns were commendable, the Council simply didn't have the resources to address them at that stage.

James[27] was a sales rep I worked with at a previous corporate job. He didn't have a sustainability background and his personal goal wasn't to save the Planet but to buy himself a Ferrari with the sales commissions he would get (except he never did). When he met clients, he had a standard pitch he had learned by heart and never failed to deliver, whether he was talking to a construction company director or a building system engineer. The pitch always featured the expression "underpinned by science". Not that it wasn't true, our work there *was* underpinned by science, but you can smell a rat when you realize that that specific expression gets repeated over and over again almost as the only reason any client should have done business with us. James left the job within a year of being appointed because he didn't hit his sales targets.

Georgina's passion for sustainability and for doing the right thing prevented her from building a rapport with her Councillors. James was driven by his personal goal and was using a cookie-cutter approach instead of developing a rapport with his prospects.

Personal values and goals prevented these two very different people from engaging with their audience and getting the results they wanted. They didn't start conversations from a place of co-creation, of *offering to help* their audiences and work together with them to find the perfect triple-win solution within the specific context – a solution that would satisfy the needs of their audience, themselves and the Planet, the silent stakeholder. Crucially, neither of them tried to understand their audience's point of view.

To understand what they should have done instead, let's look at the factors that can significantly impact our everyday communication.

---

[27] Not his real name.

Why

Here are some questions for you to consider.

Ask yourself: *What is the purpose of the communication?*

In marketing, it is well known that communication must have a purpose – usually one of education, entertainment or awareness. The same categories can be applied to your day-to-day sustainability communication.

Now ask: *Do you want to make your audience aware of something? Entertain them? Educate them?*

In the business context, additional purposes could be to get to know your audience or exchange ideas with them – probably the most powerful way to use communication and the one that can lead directly to co-creation.

Additionally, you'll want a call-to-action at the end.

Finally, ask: *What do you want your audience to do as a result of the communication?*

I suggest you never go to a meeting unless you have one to three key objectives to obtain and/or a call-to-action. If you don't have any, don't go. It will be a waste of time.

Rule 1: Have a clear purpose and a call-to-action for any communication.

Who

Here are some more questions to consider.

- *Who is speaking and who is the audience?*

- *Do they know each other?*

- *Do they belong to the same demographic group or culture?*

It is quite self-explanatory why communication is easier if there is already a relationship between the two parties and if they have something in common. Yet people forget this and go straight into a meeting or presenting the same trite slide deck without tailoring the message to the audience, because they didn't establish that all-important rapport with their audience first or researched them beforehand.

Make sure you have a few minutes before a conversation to ground yourself (perhaps with some simple breathing exercises or by stepping outside) and gather thoughts about your audience and the goals of the conversation. For that reason, I suggest avoiding back-to-back meetings.

Small talk is often dismissed as something pointless when, in fact, a 10-minute conversation with another person before starting a meeting can be a moment of insight into someone else's life and state of mind. It might lead to a real connection. Just think of the profound conversations happening on night flights with complete strangers or at some serendipitous networking event when we don't know anybody.

If you don't research and don't know your audience, you might, for example, use metaphors that are tied to a certain culture and not universally understood – a British professional using cricket's rules as an example of business practices in Italy will get back... crickets, since this is not a sport that is played much over there.

It is also useful to try to get an idea of the *personality of your audience*. Often, we lead with *our perspective*, not our audience's. "What's wrong with that," you'll ask?

When entering a delicate negotiation, hostage negotiators immediately try to step into their counterpart's shoes to understand their mindset and emotional makeup. This gives them an advantage because then they'll know what's important for the other person and can leverage that to build rapport and influence them.

If we do the same, we can talk about turning a profit with sustainability (if that's what your audience is interested in) instead of leading from the ethical perspective, and adjust our communication style and language accordingly.

But how do you get the personality of your audience if you are not a psychologist or mind reader? Figure 3 shows a simple method of obtaining a rough idea of their personality traits – and therefore their preferred communication style. It's called the DISC (Dominant, Influential, Steady and Compliant) assessment.[28]

---

[28] Everything DiSC® | Knowledge & Resources (2024, August 26). www.discprofiles.com/

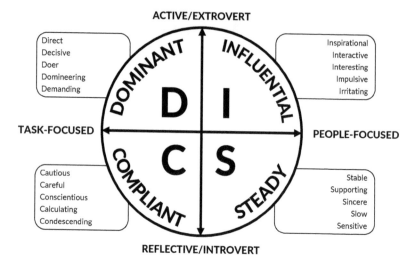

Figure 3 *The DISC personalities and alternative ways of defining the four main traits*

A word of caution, though: it would be naive to assume that billions of people on the Planet fall into four simple categories. I, myself, am a combination of the four DISC personalities and display traits of each depending on the situation and audience I'm dealing with. However, this tool can be a useful rule of thumb to use when planning what arguments and style of communication would land best with someone you are about to meet.

As an example, a busy *Dominant* executive will want brief, to-the-point communication, better if face to face, and they will want to know immediately what's in it for them. Long and convoluted emails won't do. And while you can't ask your clients or bosses to take an assessment before speaking with them, often these traits will be evident in their written and spoken communication style.[29] If you have exchanged emails before the meeting, or spoken on the phone, you might already have an idea of their personality. In particular, we are interested to find out whether they seem extroverted or introverted and whether they prefer to focus on tasks and data versus people.

---

[29] I suggest you make this a game for yourself to get familiar with the tool: guess the DISC personality from people's way of talking, walking, gesticulating and even LinkedIn profile pictures!

A combination of being extroverted/active and people-focused, for instance, will result in your audience being *Influential*. This type of personality tends to focus their energies on catalysing people around themselves and on the bigger picture rather than the details. When you speak with *Influential* personalities, you shouldn't jump straight into work mode and the task at hand. Better to have a friendly chat and ask some questions about them, then you can paint the big picture and talk about what new opportunities connected to sustainability will make them (and their companies) stand out in the market, attract talent and win awards. At no point will they be interested in *how* to achieve any of that. Someone else in the company with a *Compliant* personality will be the person taking care of the details.

For a *Compliant* person, it's all about the minutiae and managing risks since they tend to have an introverted personality focused on tasks rather than people, and generally love data.

Finally, a *Steady* person tends to be introverted and cares about others. Talking about the positive impact of integrating sustainability on people and the Planet will be a winning argument with them.[30]

In Figure 4, you'll find the type of *winning sustainability benefits* relevant to the various personality types.[31]

Rule 2: Get to know your audience. Research them beforehand. Find common ground whenever you can. Embrace small-talk moments before starting a meeting.

---

[30] The perfect example of why talking about money is not always the best influencing strategy!

[31] This was first published in my previous book, *SustainABLE: How to Find Success as a Sustainability Professional in a Rapidly Changing World* (2020).

	AUDIENCE'S PERSONALITY	YOUR COMMUNICATION STYLE	WINNING SUSTAINABILITY BENEFITS	DO	AVOID
DOMINANT	Direct, decisive, doer, domineering	Fast and energetic, big picture approach, face-to-face, to-the-point	Return on investment, cost savings, competitive advantage, productivity	Provide solutions not opinions, solicit (and expect) immediate action, show tangible benefits, use logic	Small talk, lengthy emails, fluffy arguments
INFLUENTIAL	Inspirational, interactive, impulsive	Personal, positive and imaginative approach, open and enthusiastic	New opportunities, inspirational views, market differentiation, brand awareness, attracting talent, risk management	Summarize the key points and ask them to commit to a plan, show how (high profile) others have done it successfully, allow them to think aloud and change their mind	Too much detail, formal or rigid approach
STEADY	Stable, supportive, sincere, slow	Steady and personal talk, focus on values and areas of agreement	Positive impact on people and the Planet, long-term security/resilience, attracting talent, risk management	Show sincere interest, build the relationship, deliver on promises, send info in advance, allow for reflection time, minimize risks	Fast action, pushing for an immediate response, burdening them with impersonal data
COMPLIANT	Cautious, careful, conscientious, calculating	Business-like, logical and structured	Technical advantages, risk management, long-term security/resilience, due diligence	Prepare in advance, provide plenty of details and logical arguments, be direct, allow for reflection time	Imprecision and fluffy arguments, excessive extroversion, pushing for an immediate response

***Figure 4** Winning sustainability benefits relevant to the various DISC personality types*

Strategic communication: tailoring messages to different personality types in meetings

Amit A is the Head of ESG and Sustainability at a medium design and construction company.

I recently used the Good Communicator framework for an internal meeting with the Managing Partner and Project Coordinator of my company. In the meeting we discussed how to present two potential environmental certification schemes to an important client.

I had never given much consideration to what content and style of communication would appeal to other people in a meeting.

My natural inclination, as a technical person and keen environmentalist, would have previously been to just look at the technical advantages and disadvantages of the two certification schemes and perhaps some ethical considerations but this would have left me unprepared for the inevitable questions about profit that the Managing Partner asked.

By using this framework, and the DISC personality tool within it, I realized that the Managing Partner has an evident *Dominant* personality, as he's more interested in the economics of our work than its sustainability impacts.

The Project Coordinator shows a *Compliant* personality, demonstrated by his attention to details and technical focus.

By studying their personalities and establishing what I wanted to get out of the meeting beforehand, I was able to bring to the table sufficient economic and technical evidence that would appeal to both people – ethical considerations would not have resonated with either, so I left them out.

As a result of having presented my thoughts in line with what I knew would appeal to each of the attendees, my proposed strategy for approaching our client was accepted and I came across not only as technically sound but also as a commercially credible leader.

In the future, I will always make sure I prepare for meetings by having sufficient data and evidence to appeal to different audience's personalities as this has proven a successful strategy.

The purpose and audience will also dictate the following points: what and how.

What and how

The purpose of this book is to focus on one-to-one or one-to-many, mostly verbal, communication. But, as you know, this is only a part of the complex communication ecosystem and it might not always be the best way to convey your messages. Often meetings get called just to make people aware of something. Obviously, if we want to communicate a substantial change to the way the company will operate from now on, it is better to have a meeting to gather people's feedback and questions. And if there is a genuine need to involve others and exchange ideas, meetings or focused workshops with a few relevant people are much better than emails. That said, if we want to communicate that our T&Cs have changed… an email will do.

Some recent research tells us that the average employee spends 21.5 hours in meetings every week and attends 62 meetings every month; US businesses waste an average of US$37 billion a year on unnecessary meetings.[32] Meetings are by nature the best way to gather people's opinions, ask questions and craft something together, rather than unilaterally convey information.

If we want to raise awareness over a complex issue that will substantially affect the whole company (for instance, a new sustainability policy), this can be done as a more comprehensive communication campaign, made up of breakfast meetings, posters, emails and so on.

---

[32] McCain, A. (2023, May 12). 25+ Wasting time at work Statistics [2023]: How much time is wasted at work. Zippia. www.zippia.com/advice/wasting-time-at-work-statistics/

When I was made redundant from my corporate job before founding Green Gorilla, my boss communicated my colleagues' and my redundancy to the whole division in a public meeting before telling us in private. A clear and painful example of the wrong communication medium for that particular message.

This hopefully demonstrates that the *how* is just as important as the *what* – the message itself – to land and have the desired effect on the audience and, as such, it needs to be carefully considered.

Rule 3: Consider how your communication can best take place. Having considered the purpose and audience, ask: *Is a meeting the best way, or would an email do? Do you need a whole communication campaign, or would a moment in the kitchen while making coffee suffice?*

When and where

In the previous example, my boss chose not only the wrong medium but also the wrong place and time. He knew I was going through a difficult personal time and he didn't take that into account. That public broadcast annihilated me. It's important to tune in with your audience and understand their emotional status before starting a conversation in which you want to get a positive response or a buy-in. Here is where switching on your empathy antennae will pay off. Does the person seem "off"? A gentle question might help clarify their current state of mind and help you decide whether that's the best time to talk.

The place you choose for a conversation is also important. A busy café might be great for getting to know someone and having a casual conversation, but might not be the best for a serious conversation that might change the course of a company's future.

Rule 4: Consider the environment in which the communication takes place and the state of mind of the other person at this point in time.

Shifting mindsets

Back to my reflection on hostage negotiators. These professionals know that their audience is made of troubled, extremely unpredictable and dangerous individuals.[33] A negotiator's approach is always to get to know them first and to introduce themselves as peers by using their own and the counterpart's first names. They don't have a rigid script or a "negotiator pitch" because it all depends on the individuals' personalities and specific situations.

What negotiators know well and always have to keep at the front of their minds, though, is that these are desperate people, ready to pull a trigger without notice, and that emotions run high.

For these reasons, hostage negotiators take time to listen. Sometimes, a very long time. This shows they take into consideration the *Relatedness* and *Status* needs of their counterparts. They don't try to anger them, belittle them or tell them what to do right away – it would be too dangerous to show them a lack of respect. Negotiators demonstrate with their measured actions, and a calm and low tone of voice, that they understand the other person's concerns. Note that this doesn't mean they agree with them, but that they understand where they are coming from.

This approach is called *tactical empathy* and, as change-making leaders, we can learn a lot from that. How often do you feel you are run by your

---

[33] If you want to know more about the negotiation techniques of FBI negotiators, you can take a look at Voss, C. (2016). *Never Split the Difference*; and Noesner, G. (2010). *Stalling for Time.*

emotions as opposed to by your brain in a meeting because the other person has different values from you or is brushing over your ideas?

Some of us are also particularly sensitive to rejection and the heat of the moment for a couple of reasons, as follows.

- Technical experts are rarely trained in sales. Salespeople are used to being rejected, but they quickly learn to reframe a "no" as a "no for now" and just move on to the next potential client without even blinking.

- Sustainability may be a value for us – central to who we are and who we want to be – and every time our values are negated or ignored, we can have a very emotional reaction and take it personally.[34]

But if we rationally dissect our reaction to people having different opinions from us, giving us negative feedback or rejecting our ideas, we can start to change our behaviour when the issue presents itself again. We become aware of the fact that we can be prone to become emotional, or angry.

You may ask: *But how can I change my instinctive reactions?*

People are deliciously emotional. It's what makes us human, right? Emotions play a key role in the way business is conducted. Hollywood movies convince us that we must have nerves of steel and that people make astute and calculated decisions on the spot. Reality is very different. Business is a subtle dance of emotions and, if you are dealing with sustainability, even more.

So, let's look at the role of your and your audience's emotional state in difficult situations and how to deal with it: understanding and regulating emotions will allow you to influence others more easily.[35]

---

[34] Some of us can suffer also from a recognized condition called Rejection Sensitivity Dysphoria, especially neurodivergent folks, which can make rejection an extremely painful experience.

[35] I want to stress here that the techniques outlined in this book must be used ethically. You don't want to con anyone to do something that goes against their own interest and principles. The idea is to influence others to work with you towards a positive outcome for them, you and the Planet.

Let's start from your own mindset

Imagine you are in a meeting that is not going well. The person in front of you is denying the Earth is spherical or that climate change is human-made or something less drastic that still provokes a strong reaction in you. You know that getting angry will work against you in the negotiation. A proven technique to overcome extreme emotional reactions when they are unwanted is to stop yourself in your tracks and try to read what's going on inside you. Let's understand where and how all of this is taking place.

Welcome to your wonderful brain.

In the 1960s, American neuroscientist Paul MacLean proposed the triune brain model,[36] dividing the human brain into three regions based on an evolutionary perspective, as follows.

Figure 5 *The triune brain: lizard, mouse and human*

1. **Reptilian or primal brain (basal ganglia):** the first to form through evolution, it's responsible for primal instincts and focused on avoiding harm. This has been renamed by neuropsychologist Rick Hanson the "reptile or lizard brain".[37]

[36] MacLean, P. (1990). *The Triune Brain in Evolution. Role in Paleocerebral Functions.* xxiv, illus. Science.

[37] Hanson, R. (2020, May 25). *How the brain evolved.* Psychology Today. www.psychologytoday.com/us/blog/your-wise-brain/202005/how-the-brain-evolved

2. **Paleomammalian or emotional brain (limbic system):** manages emotions and the affective system and therefore focuses on "feeding" you (emotionally, physically, even spiritually); this is your "mammal or mouse brain".
3. **Neomammalian or rational brain (neocortex):** handles rational and objective thought – your "human" brain.

When we have a strong, instinctive reaction without much thought, it's the "lizard" brain that acts first. Then the "mouse" brain, when your raw emotions start to surface. These ancient parts of your brain want to keep you safe and can be up to 20 times faster than your "human" brain, which means that, to regain clarity and emotional control, you have to press the pause button.

This can be done in a few simple stages, as follows.

1. Slow down

Remove yourself from the situation if it's all too much or, at the very least, breathe deeply and elongate the exhalation to allow your neocortex to catch up and start rationalizing the situation. A very helpful breathing technique is the "physiological sigh", discovered in the 1930s and recently brought to wider fruition by Dr Andrew Huberman:[38] a pattern of breathing of two inhales followed by an extended exhale. You can also try to focus your attention on any of your senses. For example:

- rub two fingers slowly so that you can feel the ridges on them and all the sensations that surface

- close your eyes and listen attentively to the sounds around you without judgement, from the furthest to the closest, and/or

- observe in exquisite detail whatever is in front of you, noticing the light, colours, patterns and textures. If you become distracted, gently pull your mind away from those thoughts and come back to observing.

---

[38] Huberman, A. (2021, April 7). Reduce Anxiety & Stress with the Physiological Sigh | Huberman Lab Quantal Clip [Video]. YouTube. www.youtube.com/watch?v=rBdhqBGqiMc

In essence, in order to slow down your racing mind it will help to "drop into" your body and "ground" yourself.

2. Notice your body and physiological reactions

What are you feeling? Are you sweating? Is your pulse racing? Can you feel yourself blushing or do you have a pit in your stomach? Do you feel like crying? Any unusual physical manifestation will be an indication that something is going on.

3. Try to label your negative emotions without judgement

These may be fear, surprise, sadness, disgust, frustration, shame, anger. Pay attention to the negative emotions you experience more often than others. This might be an indication of your brain's preferred way of reacting to a trigger as a form of self-defence from perceived harm, developed as you were growing up.[39] For instance, every time someone ignores your instructions, you might get incredibly frustrated and can't shake that feeling off. That could be an indication that you have a controller, perfectionist or hyper-achieving personality trait. These personality traits might have developed over time to help you overcome a fear of failure or disorientating chaos while growing up. If you pay close attention to your train of thought, you may also identify the negative and damning narrative that is behind your reactions – perhaps that you are not good enough.

While these strong negative emotions were perhaps helpful to address immediate perceived threats when you were growing up, they are not any more if they make you feel miserable and lose agency over the circumstances. In fact, they become "saboteurs" which prevent you from achieving your full potential.[40]

---

[39] Frey, S. (2022). *The Neuroscience of Positive Intelligence*. https://web.positiveintelligence.com/neuroscience-white-paper

[40] These concepts have been developed over centuries, and are familiar in Buddhism. If you wish to identify more clearly your usual negative reactions, or "saboteurs", you can read Chamine, S. (2012). *Positive Intelligence: Why Only 20% of Teams and Individuals Achieve Their True Potential and How You Can Achieve Yours*. Alternatively, take the Positive Intelligence saboteurs assessment: www.positiveintelligence.com/saboteurs/

When you are able to identify your emotions, and slow down by "grounding" yourself, you regain your power and ability to think straight. You are creating a buffer and a healthy distance from the feelings that consume you and activate the lizard part of your brain's fight, flight or freeze response.

4. Assess your situation

Now that you have calmed down and hopefully identified the most common ways you self-sabotage and react to triggers, you can look at the situation in a wiser way. You can consciously think about what helpful qualities you'd need to employ in the current situation, perhaps:

- empathy towards yourself and others

- curiosity, to engage more meaningfully with others and the situation

- flexible and innovative thinking, and

- optimism and decisiveness to go from words to action.

5. Reframe the situation

It's not the person in front of you that's the barrier, it's the issue. We are so used to being at each other's throats when opinions diverge that we forget we are in it together. The Earth's systems collapse we are facing can affect the rich and poor, people of any gender speaking any language, and every country around the globe without discrimination. So, let's try to step out of the room where the bad meeting is happening, think that we are fellow humans and *we can* find commonalities that will help us connect and take the conversation to another level.

6. Bury the hatchet and embark on a voyage of discovery

Nobody likes to be attacked and pushed to do anything. Newton's Third Law of Motion states that for every action there is an equal and opposite reaction – a physics law that affects not only moving objects but also our way of reacting to triggers. If you attack someone directly, or push them to do something they don't want to do, you can only expect an equally strong opposite reaction.

But if you *de-personalize the issue*, become curious about someone's point of view and focus on resolving the issue *together* with them, like a puzzle, you'll have a bigger chance of being successful: you'll have put a healthy distance between you and the issue, allowing your brain's rational neocortex to find a logical solution rather than being swayed by your "lizard brain".

What's more, you'll have formed a rapport with your audience in which both of you have equal power to change the status quo towards a triple-win situation.

7. Develop your resilience

Even if working in sustainability is not a war, you need to develop your resilience over time – because it's a marathon, not a sprint. Otherwise, you'll end up burning out.

When my clients come to me feeling stressed and hopeless, sometimes it feels patronizing to ask them how well they are sleeping, whether they are spending time outdoors or what their diet looks like. After all, we are all adults and we know we should exercise and eat healthily. However, I still ask these questions, because I know plenty of people that hustle so much that they forget to eat. Neglecting our basic human needs leads to chronic stress until our bodies go into survival mode. And when we are in that physical and psychological state, we prioritize comfort in the form of chocolate and wine and avoid the gym or walking outside.

This is what our lizard brain is telling us to do in order to conserve energy when, rationally, we know that a healthier lifestyle has the power to lower the risk of depression and a range of physical illnesses. Go back to basics and think about the nine Fs[41] in Figure 6. Starting at the base of the pyramid, you need to make sure you are giving these spheres of your life daily attention, especially the basic ones. Your body and mind are your main instruments to make a difference in the world, and they need regular maintenance and attention.

---

[41] Adapted from *Diane Wilkinson's 10F Spring Model*. EMCC Global (2024, March 28). Diane Wilkinson – Building Resilience: Impact of 10F Spring model [Video]. YouTube. www.youtube.com/watch?v=SavkEkYtljs; and *Maslow's Hierachy of Needs*. Copley, L., PhD (2024, August 16). Hierarchy of Needs: A 2024 Take on Maslow's Findings. PositivePsychology.com. https://positivepsychology.com/hierarchy-of-needs/

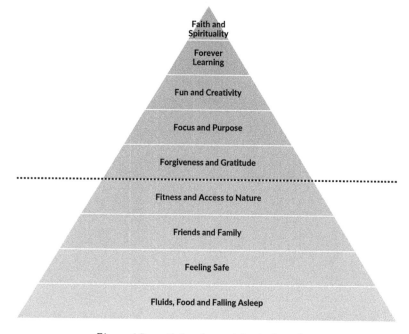

Figure 6 *Pyramid of needs, essential to develop resilience*

How about other people's mindset?

Once you have regained control over your emotions, shift your attention to your audience. By doing so, you'll be able to deepen your understanding of their feelings and needs, and formulate an appropriate response.

Note that you don't need to agree with them or fight them, but to activate the FBI negotiator's *tactical empathy*, which consists of listening on steroids.

Listen attentively and activate all the empathy you have within you to understand the other person's feelings, thoughts and behaviours – not to agree with them, but to respond accordingly. Only then can you work together to co-create solutions.

It is an immense act of compassion to try to understand someone else's world, especially someone you dislike or who has a radically different opinion from yours.

It won't be easy, as you'll need to set your pride and rightful attitude aside and connect at a human level by asking open questions and listening to their answers fully, while refraining from interrupting. Instead of waiting impatiently to speak, and listing in your head all your counter-arguments, active listening implies making a conscious effort to allow the other person to fully share their thoughts and try to understand them. A good way to ensure you have understood their message correctly is to reflect back on it by formulating statements such as: "*It looks like* you need to progress this project quickly" or "*It sounds like* it has been quite hard to address this issue so far."[42]

Ask yourself: *What does it feel like to see life from their perspective?* The more they will feel understood and listened to, the more they will feel connected to you and trust you.

And while you might have heard about these communication techniques in management courses, there is an additional reason why they are key in sustainability: sustainability can be perceived very differently by different people. It can be political (when, for instance, sustainability is adopted in a company just as a marketing move and ends up in greenwashing) or a very personal subject (think about those who lost their homes and livelihood to flooding or wildfires), but, more importantly, it can also be as I mentioned earlier, part of people's value sets – hence the strong emotional reactions.

For some of your clients and board members, it can be nothing more than "Any other business" at the end of their agendas. The urgency of it all might not have landed for them yet or they might feel like it's someone else's business, and this can clash wildly against your own, emotionally charged reaction to it, giving your counterpart the upper hand in the negotiations.

How can I influence other people's behaviours?

FBI negotiators and experienced salespeople know that they must focus on emotions to influence others' behaviour. Data and percentages alone have zero impact and do not change behaviours.

---

[42] In this second example, you are also acknowledging their feelings, which is always a pleasant experience for the person in front of you, as they will feel understood.

In my experience, the most preparation sustainability professionals do before a new client meeting or presenting to a board is to put together a slide deck full of data, percentages and facts, including how sustainability is the right or the ethical thing to do. We might throw in how wonderful our company is as well. But think about all the most successful manufacturers of consumer goods and how they rarely spend precious advertising airtime to list the characteristics of their products. Rather, they show the *lifestyle* you'd have if you bought their products.

Apple's "Think different" slogan conveyed the fact that users of Apple products are unique and different from others. Apple's ads are all about style and exciting, high-end performance. They mostly focus on why people should buy their products and how these align with a sophisticated lifestyle, not on their products' specifications.

I imagine that when global media and tech company Bloomberg decided to commission the world's most sustainable office building at the time,[43] they were convinced by the prospect of breathing fresh, pure air in the middle of the City; by the idea of being on every design magazine's front cover for months on end; by the thought of having an ultramodern yet healthy and beautiful building, in which employees would be inspired to work, while aesthetically fitting in with the existing buildings in the area.

It also made perfect business sense, from getting massive positive publicity and a reputation boost to attracting the best talent. The vision behind a complex and costly project like that would have been about how it would *feel* to its future users. The details of how that ground-breaking air filtering system worked were the engineers' concern, not the client's.

Similarly, if you want to sell sustainability to someone, you'd need to explain how sustainability can improve and enhance their lifestyle. What would their life look like if they embraced it?

---

[43] Their HQ in London, which was inaugurated in 2017 and received the highest BREEAM (Building Research Establishment Environmental Assessment Method) score ever: 98.5%. The building was designed to have a sophisticated natural ventilation system that supplies fresh outdoor air to Bloomberg's 4,500 employees in the heart of London.

The thought of having cosy winter nights at home with their families is likely to provoke a stronger positive reaction in homeowners than just listing the technical characteristics of an air source heat pump.

This is often called *storytelling*:[44] the human brain is wired to learn via stories and imagery, rather than pure data, and it is ignited by interest. Moreover, people use their guts to make decisions, not their brains – and stories have the power to trigger those emotions and shift a negotiation.

Facts are used only as corroborating evidence by most to justify retrospectively their instinctive decisions. Therefore, the more you manage to make your interactions as interesting and relatable as possible for your specific audience, the more their emotional response will be positive, with the consequence that they will trust you and listen to you – whether or not they have access to the full data set.

Naturally, not everyone was born to tell stories – and most of us lost the ability to create imaginary scenarios when we grew up. You might be more of a technical person and prefer data and facts rather than the "fluffiness" of stories. Of course, those of us who can paint a potential future in technicolour might come across as more charismatic.

But mostly, it is possible to get the audience to listen to you more attentively by simply:

- sharing a good case study, complete with challenges, winning strategies and lessons learned

- using props (perhaps the product/material you are suggesting they adopt)

- offering the direct experiences of others who have gone through something similar via recorded videos or in person

- offering your audience the opportunity to visit places that relate closely to their situation so that they can have a more immersive experience, and finally

---

[44] I know there will be some of you ready to roll their eyes when they hear "storytelling", since it has become a buzzword in recent years; at the same time, it's not always used correctly or to its full power. In this book, I use the term to indicate a better way to, mainly, craft case studies so that they can become a useful tool in your effective communication toolbox.

- sprinkling a few elements of surprise and entertainment while presenting it – some light humour can go a long way.

Finding out what makes people tick

In Part 1, we saw how, unless a threat feels personal and impending, we don't act. Also, people do not pay attention to boring stuff (no pressure for me here!), so you'll need to keep their attention high with topics that are interesting, close to their heart and immediately useful to them. This is why it is so important to get curious about what your audience cares about and what their most urgent needs and wants are.

Without this knowledge, you cannot sell them sustainability effectively because you wouldn't be able to paint a vivid picture of what's in it for them and their future – besides the ethical and moral argument, which, we have seen, does not work for everybody.

How can you find out what your audience cares about, then? There are two main ways: (1) doing your homework, and (2) adopting a coaching approach.

1. Doing your homework

A quick search on your audience's public profiles online before meeting them can often do the trick. People often share their ideas, likes and dislikes publicly and candidly without much thought. Imagine you were doing some market research on your audience and what's called a *market segmentation profiling* on them. Ask yourself some questions while researching them online.[45]

- **Demographic:** *Who are they? What are their preferred pronouns? How old are they? What is their education level? Do they have a family? What's their job role?*

---

[45] An important disclaimer here: this exercise is purely to try to better understand the person you will have a conversation with, not to stereotype them or make assumptions based on your own views of life. While it's helpful to "profile" them to tailor your language and message accordingly, always keep an open mind and embrace any conversation with curiosity.

- **Behaviours:** *What do they do? What habits do they have? What are their likes and dislikes towards a certain issue (e.g. sustainability)? What do they value?*

- **Geographic:** *Where are they located?*

- **Psychographic:** *What do they believe in? What do they think? What is their perception of a certain reality (e.g. sustainability)?*

I invite you to do a similar exercise on their companies, as the combination of the two will provide you with rich information that will help you communicate more effectively. But remember that we always interact with human beings and that person-to-person relationships are key to developing corporate relationships.

2. Adopting a coaching approach

In this approach, you avoid being directive and telling people what to do, and instead, use questions to deeply understand the issues and the person in front of you. Additionally, you give your audience your full attention and the space to think. This will allow them to express their thoughts more articulately and you to get a more comprehensive idea of their wants and needs, which might uncover some factors that not even your audience knew existed!

To adopt this approach, get into the habit of asking **open questions**, those questions that don't have a single "yes" or "no" answer. Starting a question with *How…?, What…?, When…?, Why…?, Where…?* or *Who…?* will elicit more elaborate answers from your audience. As an example, instead of asking *Do you have a budget ring-fenced for sustainability?*, ask *How do you plan to finance this project?*

The first question calls for a monosyllabic answer. If you don't ask a follow-up question, this will be it and you will not have an opportunity to uncover any potential threats to the project connected to poor financial decisions, or opportunities to explore green investments and grants.

The other advantage of asking better questions is that it will increase buy-in. When the right question is asked (perhaps one that puts them against their illogical reasoning or the potential losses they will suffer if they don't adopt sustainability), their answer will be more powerful than being told what to do – which causes an opposite reaction, as we have seen. The audience will effectively convince themselves that sustainability is all they need.

A coaching approach also implies **listening fully and actively** to the answer your audience provides. This means:

- no gazing at mobile phones or other tech unless absolutely necessary

- reassuring the audience that you are listening by nodding when appropriate and repeating their key statements for clarity

- capturing any discrepancy between their message and their body language, and gently offering these back to them; for instance: *I hear you saying that you are happy to proceed, but I can detect some nervousness. Am I right? Is there something I can explain further?*

Active listening has several advantages. It will allow you to:

- understand better and learn more about the project and your audience

- detect any potential underlying issues and opportunities

- increase your audience's trust in you. Who doesn't like someone who listens attentively? This simple act, quite surprisingly, has the potential to change your audience's brain chemistry by increasing their oxytocin levels, the "feel good" hormone which not only makes them happier but also more inclined to believe and entrust you.

Remember, all of these skills can be learned but it is necessary to practise them as often as possible to master them. So, I invite you to put down this book right now and plan in which forthcoming meeting or conversation you are going to implement the techniques you have read about so far.

What if I'm not a natural communicator?

There is a myth that you might believe yourself, that you were either born a great communicator or you were not. Of course, some of us, perhaps those more extroverted, find it easier to jump on a stage and talk to a large audience. Others can make friends even with inanimate objects – Wilson of the movie *Cast Away* comes to mind. But in general, great speakers are made, not born.

A classic example is TED Talk speakers. They are so polished that they look natural. And I'm sure you have experienced this in your own life. If you play an instrument effortlessly, how many hours of practice did you put into it to reach this point? If you can cook a delicious meal without much thought, how many dodgy student-style meals did you have to go through to get to this point? When you were born, could you drive a car?

You get the gist. To be a natural at anything, you are either really gifted or you have to put in the work. Some studies indicate that you need an average of 10,000 hours of *deliberate* practice to hone any craft.[46]

---

[46] Ericsson, K. A., Krampe, R. T. and Tesch-Römer, C. (1993). The role of deliberate practice in the acquisition of expert performance. *Psychological Review*, 100(3), 363–406. This seminal study looked at how many hours of practice violinists needed to do in order to master the instrument, and concluded that "individual differences in ultimate performance can largely be accounted for by differential amounts of past and current

Communication is not different. Of course, you can finish this book and perhaps take away a couple of key points – for instance, that you need to listen attentively and ask the right questions – but that *will not* make you a better communicator. Not if you don't practise them!!

If you want to have a chance at influencing others, I'm sorry but there is no shortcut or magic wand I can give you. You have to practise at any given opportunity: this evening, with your partner or children; tomorrow morning, with your next client; in the afternoon, over coffee with a friend. Anything goes because even though you might not be specifically talking about sustainability, you'd be honing these all-important skills, a little at a time. Paying more attention than last time, practising being present a little longer. It will be like carving out the unnecessary and revealing the beauty of your communication skills, which are already contained in you, just like Michelangelo did with his statues.

If communication is absolutely key to your role as is the case in most roles, I suggest that you push the boundaries of your comfort zone – as there is no growth within it – and run a month-long experiment: make it your mission for the next 30 days to have better conversations with people. You can keep score in a journal of how many conversations you have, with whom and how they went. Revisit the results every week and, at the end of the experiment, adjust your style and techniques as needed. Take any opportunity to initiate climate or sustainability conversations with anybody – the cashier at the supermarket, a fellow gym-goer, the librarian at your local library, and the most dreaded, your own family – not just clients or like-minded sustainability professionals. These conversations can be your playground to learn how to speak to different audiences outside your sustainability bubble which, eventually, will make you a better communicator.

An exercise I ask my clients to do during training sessions is to pretend the other person is a five-year-old child. This admittedly is easier for

---

levels of practice". The "10,000 hours of practice to reach mastery" shared in the study was popularized by author Malcolm Gladwell in his book *Outliers* (2008), becoming almost the benchmark for honing any craft, but later criticized by others. The takeaway here should be: you need many hours of intentional practice to hone any skills, unless you have a natural talent for it.

parents, as they have already developed the capacity to speak in simple terms with their children, but anyone can benefit from this eye-opening task. I invite them to explain a sustainability concept, like sustainable development or circular economy, to this child. You will need to adjust your language to make it easier to understand and eliminate any jargon, and perhaps slow down your speaking pace.

As an example, take the definition of circular economy given by the Ellen McArthur Foundation:

> The circular economy is a system where materials never become waste and nature is regenerated. In a circular economy, products and materials are kept in circulation through processes like maintenance, reuse, refurbishment, remanufacture, recycling, and composting. The circular economy tackles climate change and other global challenges, like biodiversity loss, waste, and pollution, by decoupling economic activity from the consumption of finite resources.[47]

For a sustainability professional, there is nothing incomprehensible there. But would a child understand "regenerated", "kept in circulation" or "refurbishment"? I have two of those little people and the answer is: no, they wouldn't.

Now look, by comparison, at how sustainability professional and illustrator Alex Magnin explains this concept in one of his brilliant YouTube videos:

> Circular economy means that everything is healthy food for something else.

This clever definition was given by his wife to their three-year-old child.[48] Everyone can benefit from rethinking the terminology they use in conversations. You might not have a child covered in jam in front of you, but a businesswoman in a suit; that doesn't mean that you can assume she understands everything you are saying. She might

---

[47] Circular economy introduction (n.d.). Ellen MacArthur Foundation. www.ellenmacarthurfoundation.org/topics/circular-economy-introduction/overview

[48] *Circular Economy: definition & examples* (2020, December 16). Sustainability Illustrated. https://sustainabilityillustrated.com/en/portfolio/circular-economy-definition-examples/

have an MBA and know absolutely nothing about "regeneration" or "decoupling economic activity from the consumption of finite resources". Without being patronizing, paying attention to what your audience might understand and what they might not is key to successful communication.[49]

In fact, *paying attention* is the *one thing* that will make you a better communicator.

When I was a teenager in Italy a book came out, which became popular very quickly: *Va Dove Ti Porta il Cuore*.[50] As it happens, I can't remember the storyline or the characters, but I do remember a sentence, which I even hung on my bedroom wall for years:

L'amore é attenzione. (Love is attention.)

Simple. But so true.

When you pay attention to someone, you demonstrate how important they are to you. When you don't, even if you love them, you are communicating that they are not important to you. Paying attention is the key to any successful interaction with people and, ultimately, to any successful relationship. Being fully present makes others feel important, appreciated and heard. Showing genuine interest in the other person lowers their barriers and makes them more likely to trust you and listen to you.

I know you are in this business because of your values. And if this feels like having to fake interest, it will also feel cunning. However, I'm not asking you to fake anything but to open up to the fact that *any* person is inherently worth paying attention to and that, additionally, they might have something important to share with you.

---

[49] Recently, a coaching client told me that she didn't feel impactful in meetings as she felt intimidated by some of her own clients: they would use jargon from their own industry she wouldn't understand, but she believed she would come across as incompetent if she asked for any explanation. Without realizing, she was going through that same experience she was probably putting others through. If this has been your experience as well, hopefully you can see the flip side, empathize with your clients and do something about it!

[50] By novelist Susanna Tamaro, translated into English with the title *Follow Your Heart* (1994).

Even if you are not a natural communicator, you can always start the conversation with the intention of establishing a connection. And giving your audience a chance to become your partner in co-creating a better future, even if they seem against the idea to start with.

You might feel nervous about talking to them; if that's the case, you can go back to the grounding techniques shared at the start of Part 2 to slow down your lizard brain.

Here is another wonderful, quick grounding exercise that also helps to facilitate the connection with others.[51]

- Inhale and feel the elongation of your spine in a "noble", dignified posture.

- Exhale and soften and, while you do that, think of someone who makes you smile and feel the warmth: you'll feel "shiny".

- Finally expand your "awesome" warm bubble to include the audience with compassion.

Most importantly, don't underestimate the power of Nature to ground you before an important meeting. A few minutes in a quiet natural environment, just observing what's going on without narrative or judgement, noticing sounds, sights, smells and sensations, and a few deep breaths, will have a wonderful calming effect on the body and the mind.

---

[51] Coach Wendy Palmer in her *A Touch of Grace* speech (Leadership Embodiment (2016, February 16). *Wendy Palmer – A Touch of Grace* [Video]. YouTube. www.youtube.com/watch?v=O-yPDozALwg) defines it as an exercise to embody your own noble, shiny and awesome self.

How does communication change from conversations to presentations?

This book is all about conversations, but what if instead of one-to-one conversations, you have to deal with presentations with a larger audience? How do you apply the techniques I covered so far?

Presentations tend to be monologues in most cases. Someone presents to a silent audience, then asks if there are any questions, steps down from the stage and that's it.

Have you changed people's minds when this happens? Most likely, not, unless you are one of the most brilliant aforementioned TED speakers and have honed your craft really well. But what, besides rehearsing the presentation, makes TED Talks so compelling?

There are a few important elements in those that you can replicate in your own presentations and that can make all the difference.

A conversational approach to presentations

First of all, try to *imagine your presentation as a dialogue* with your audience so that you are interacting with them, not just conveying a message. If you cannot take comments and questions on the go (that's often not possible), pre-empt any potential ones the audience may have. Not sure if you have noticed, but this is what I'm doing as I write this book. I try to imagine you, my beloved reader, interacting with the content and asking questions or making comments. The hope is that, like some of the readers of my previous book, *SustainABLE*, you'll think: *Gosh, she is reading my mind!*

Attempt to take a voyage in your audience's mind and imagine what they are thinking, how they are reacting to each piece of information you share, and weave that into your presentation. Ask yourself: *How will my audience react to this particular example? Will they know what I mean?*

It will help make your presentation a lot more relevant to your audience. But the only way to do that is to know your audience well. This is obviously easier if you have only one person you are speaking to rather than a vast audience, but you can still guess their general preferences and interests. For instance, if you are speaking in front of an audience full of engineers you can guess most will fall within the DISC's *Compliant* category. They will be interested in facts and data and perhaps less in esoteric arguments.[52]

Engaging your audience with stories, data and visuals

Once you have nailed your audience, you can use the strongest tool in your toolbox: *stories*. Every great TED talk starts with a story that gets the immediate attention of the audience because it makes the content more relatable on a human level and more memorable than just sharing facts and data.

Since we are talking about sustainability, which in most cases has a scientific foundation, I suggest you start with a **case study**, typically left at the bottom of slide decks.

---

[52] As you do your homework and research your audience beforehand, you could also build a *persona* based on the market segmentation profiling discussed earlier. A *persona* in marketing is a semi-fictional representation of your ideal customer based on market research and real data about your existing customers. Personas help businesses understand and relate to their customers by encapsulating the behaviours, goals, challenges, and buying patterns of different segments of their target audience. Pearce, B. (2024, August 25). *What is a persona in marketing? Buyer & user personas explained.* Product Marketing Alliance. www.productmarketingalliance.com/your-guide-to-personas/

Perform an adult version of *show and tell*, and illustrate your idea via a practical demonstration of when it was successful in the past, before talking about the nitty-gritty of it.

I suggest you also take on board what author Brent Dykes says:

> When you present data with a narrative, you explain. When you combine data with visuals, you enlighten. When you combine visuals with narrative, you engage, but real change happens when you combine all three.[53]

Well-constructed case studies featuring **data**, **narrative** and **visual elements** offer an unforgettable and immersive experience for any audience. Here are a few examples.

- The *Atlas of Sustainable Development Goals* (SDGs) showcases the global progress for each SDG using interactive graphics that can be explored in different ways (by country, by topic, by year, etc.).

- *Information is Beautiful* is a website whose creator, David McCandless, sets out to explain, distil and clarify information about how the world works using colourful infographics that tell a story.

- The amusing and truly illuminating TED Talk *The Best Stats You've Ever Seen* by Hans Rosling, who narrates relatively dry global statistics about life expectancy vs. family size over time like a sports commentator, provoking an enthusiastic reaction from the audience.[54]

As explained earlier, the case studies have to be *relevant* to the audience.

If you are talking to CEOs, showcasing other companies that have made big shifts to incorporate sustainability to realize their vision will work. But it will not if your audience is made of engineers or facility managers. Those people will probably be more interested in a building project you have worked on, and they will appreciate being shown the technical details of a new carbon calculation tool that might make their lives easier when having to report on carbon emissions.

---

[53] Dykes, B. (2020). *Effective Data Storytelling: How to Drive Change with Data, Narrative, and Visuals.*

[54] Rosling, H. (2006). *The best stats you've ever see.* [Video]. TED Talks. www.ted.com/talks/hans_rosling_the_best_stats_you_ve_ever_seen

The key questions are, as for any other communication:

What is the purpose of this presentation? What do you want them to do at the end of it?

But also:

Why should these people give up their time to listen to you? What's in it for them?

Structuring presentations for diverse audiences

When you have to present to a variety of audiences, or when you don't know who will be sitting in front of you (for instance, at conferences), you might want to structure your presentation so that it creates an element of interest for any personality type.

- **Start with the *big ideas*.** What are the key takeaways you want your audience to have? These will appeal especially to vision-driven *Dominant* and *Influential* people.

- Then, **talk about the concrete *results* sustainability can provide**. These should appeal to anyone, but in particular, *Compliant* and *Dominant* people.

- Then **share what these ideas will mean for *people***: this will generate interest in people-oriented personalities, like *Influential* and *Steady*.

- Finally, **share some *details***, to provide credibility for *Compliant* and *Steady* personalities.

Slides: friends or foe?

There is plenty of advice out there on how to make sure your audience doesn't suffer "death by PowerPoint". What I want to add here is that you need to be aware of a potentially hostile and time-poor audience, with a lot of preconceptions and doubts about sustainability. So, the simpler the message, the easier it will be to deliver, the more incisive it will be. But a first important question to ask yourself is: *Do I need slides?*

You have a lot of choice of tools these days from PowerPoints to Notion boards to videos. But besides the choice of tools, it is important to establish whether you need *a tool* at all, or whether you can present to an audience with just the power of your body language and voice.

The best TED Talks have no slides or, at most, a few pictures and one or two incisive words. It's all in the delivery.

Don't use presentation tools as Linus' security blankets. They should enhance your message and not distract people from it. So, use them consciously and sparingly.

Tools or not, I suggest you spend some time crafting the *structure* of your presentations. In addition to what I suggested in the previous paragraph:

- start with a *story* to captivate your audience

- for memorability, ideally limit your message to *three key points* you want to get across using *data, visuals and narrative* (if you are using a presentation tool, use as few words as possible)

- eliminate or clearly explain any *jargon* and acronyms

- create opportunities for your audience to *participate actively* (via online polls, direct questions, quizzes) or use props for added interest[55]

- close with a *call-to-action*: what do you want your audience to think, say or do now?

---

[55] Learn from Bill Gates, who once took to the TED stage with a jar full of mosquitoes (which he proceeded to release) to explain the impact of malaria. Gates, B. (2009). *Mosquitos, malaria and education* [Video]. TED Talks. www.ted.com/talks/ bill_gates_mosquitos_malaria_and_education

Bringing sustainable solutions to life: props

David S is the director of a non-for-profit enterprise using Nature-based solutions to enhance biodiversity and capture carbon.

We like to take samples of fibreboard, textile and construction materials that contain elephant grass (a rapid growth plant demonstrated to capture carbon and increase biodiversity quicker than trees) to clients' meetings and presentations.

I have found that talking about renewable materials helps but there is nothing like getting your hands dirty and actually displaying the items we make!

Most importantly, prepare, prepare and prepare some more. Rehearse the presentation in front of a mirror or (if that feels cringy) use what coding engineers call *rubber duck debugging*.[56] have a rubber duck next to your screen and present it to the duck.

---

[56] Developers use this technique to debug their code by forcing themselves to explain it, line by line, to a rubber duck sitting next to their computers.

Coaching your team to communicate sustainability effectively

How developing your emotional intelligence is key to influencing others, including your team

> Emotional intelligence (EI) refers to a different way of being smart. EI is a key to high performance, particularly for outstanding leadership. It's not your IQ, but rather it's how you manage yourself and your relationships with others.
>
> *Daniel Goleman*

I firmly believe that leadership and management are two completely different concepts.

You can be an effective manager (who delivers projects on time and technically brilliant) and be an awful leader at the same time, just like you can be an effective leader without having a team that reports to you.[57] Leaders inspire. Leaders have a strong vision, care about others and can take them on their visionary journey.

---

[57] Even if you don't have a team right now, if you have passion and a vision, you can be a *thought leader* all the same. Think about change-making leaders without a team like Rosa Park or Greta Thunberg.

For maximum impact and fulfilment, I suggest you focus on being a leader. But what *kind* of leader do you want to be?[58]

Author and psychologist Daniel Goleman[59] identified five shared traits of emotionally intelligent leaders, which seems to fit perfectly with the idea of a leader who wants to maximize their own and their staff's performance in a world that is increasingly complex and challenging.

- **Self-awareness:** understanding your strengths, weaknesses, values and how you impact others.

- **Self-regulation:** controlling your impulses and emotions, and positively redirecting them.

- **Motivation:** being driven by a sense of purpose and passion.

- **Empathy:** understanding and caring about the feelings and needs of others (and your own, I would add).

- **Social skills:** communicating effectively, building relationships, and resolving conflicts.

By developing these skills, you can become the leader you want to be and when it comes to coaching your team to work more effectively and communicate sustainability, you'll be able to do a much better job.

If you are thinking that this would mean drastically changing your personality – perhaps you are an introvert and think that all of the above is the stuff of nightmares – think again. Having social skills doesn't mean over-sharing or talking all the time. It means knowing when to listen and when to talk, and how to build relationships without having to socialize with your team every week. It is (again) about *paying attention* to other people and, crucially, to the short moment between events

---

[58] Goleman talks about six main leadership styles: *Coercive Leadership Style* (Commanding, quick problem-solving); *Authoritative* (Visionary, guiding with freedom); *Affiliative* (Focus on positive environment, less directive); *Democratic* (Inclusive decision-making); *Pacesetting* (High standards, lead by example); and *Coaching* (Development-focused, one-on-one growth). They all have their pros and cons, and a wise leader flexes their style according to the specific situation and team. Goleman, D. (1998). *What Makes a Leader?* In *Best of Harvard Business Review*.

[59] Goleman, ibid.

and your reaction, so that you can make a conscious and emotionally intelligent decision with regards to what to do or say next.

You might ask at this point: *Can emotional intelligence really be learned?*

Goleman suggests there is a genetic component to emotional intelligence but there is also evidence that it can be learned and that (thankfully!) it increases with age. However, it is not as simple as going on yet another training course.

Emotional intelligence happens not in your neocortex (your "human" rational brain) but in the limbic part of the brain (the "mouse" brain), which governs emotions and feelings. This means that emotional intelligence is best learned through motivation, extended practice and feedback – not through analysis or logic. Keep in mind that coaching can be a precious tool when you don't know where to start.

A few words on vulnerability in conversations

At this point, I have to mention *vulnerability* as an important characteristic of empathic, change-making leaders.

Things are changing rapidly, but the business world is still soaked with the toxic idea that leadership equals *alpha-male* power.[60] Inflexible rules and behaviours seem to be the way to go and showing any uncertainty at work is seen as a cardinal sin that can cost you your reputation and your career. And while we are all generally more aware of mental health and perhaps secretly abhor these views, it's still hard not to feel that we have to be seen as infallible in our everyday endeavours. Paradoxically, showing our vulnerability at work takes a lot of courage.

We often lean into perfectionism and mask our true personalities, insecurities or values in the name of fitting in and being seen as perfectly consistent, just like others would expect us to be, on social media and in the office.

---

[60] Author and researcher Brené Brown, a leading expert in vulnerability, talks about the difference between *power over* others (driven by fear of losing something), *power with others* (shared power that grows out of collaboration and relationships) and *power within* (self-awareness, a key EI trait). https://brenebrown.com/hubs/dare-to-lead/

In cultures like the UK's, a "stiff upper lip" – i.e., being unemotional in the face of adversity – has been historically praised as a virtue and the opposite seen as despicable. No wonder some of us feel incredibly uncomfortable when we try to be authentic and come out of the shell we have built around us to protect our true selves.

However, leadership and power should rather be the "ability to achieve purpose and effect change", as Martin Luther King Jr. defined it.

How can we do this if we don't accept our own and our team's shortcomings as just a fact of life? If we don't promote a culture of transparency and learning from mistakes? If we don't think leaders have to serve others as opposed to be served by them? If we don't promote connection and co-creation as key tools to achieve purpose and effect change?

The big question you might be asking here is: *How can we be vulnerable* **and** *safe in conversation with others then?*

I love the BRAVING framework Brené Brown has devised for leaders, adapted here for the communication scenarios.

Boundaries: When in conversation, set healthy boundaries and invite others to do the same, clarifying what's acceptable and what's not for each individual, including what can be shared publicly. Some ground rules might be helpful, especially in sensitive conversations and with people you don't know well.

Reliability: Everyone in the conversation will commit to do what they promise during the conversation, while being aware of individual competencies, limitations and the time it takes to do the tasks at hand. Don't overpromise.

Accountability: Be brave enough to apologize and make amends if you say or do something wrong.

Vault: Do not share information that is not yours to share. Confidentiality is paramount when talking with others, so at the very least ask permission to share.

Integrity: Practise your values, even if it isn't comfortable or easy. Don't pretend to be someone else. Choose to do and say the right thing over the convenient one. Obviously, don't lie! If you don't know something, admit it but offer to look it up or ask someone else - it's all in the teamwork, remember?

Non-judgement: It's important to listen without judging, as much as humanly possible. Only by feeling not judged will other people open up to us.

Generosity: Offer to help generously, and assume others have the best intentions unless proven wrong.

Coaching your team to communicate sustainability effectively

As an effective and emotionally intelligent leader, you will want your team to become empowered and grow in their roles. This includes wanting your team to have the same ability you are acquiring to have transformational sustainability conversations. To do that you need to develop the "coach leader" in you.

Ever come across a manager who started as a brilliant technical person, then got promotion after promotion and ended up leading teams without any formal people management training (or emotional intelligence)?

I had a few in my past corporate life and, I tell you, it was hard. I worked as a sustainability consultant and most of the people I worked with were technical. They loved their facts and data (the *Compliant* type in the DISC test). So, when they were bumped into the management's driving seat, they ended up despising it. They were brilliant technical experts, which was the reason why they got promoted, rather than because they showed leadership skills. They had some *zones of genius* when it came to problem-solving a technical crisis, then questionable behaviour when it came to managing their teams – shifting between commanding and absent, and everything in between.

So, when I talk about coaching your team, I mean starting to embody emotional intelligence and act like a coach would.

But what does a coach do? They support their clients to overcome challenges and become empowered individuals by developing their *awareness, responsibility* and *choice*. They don't provide the solutions or tell people what to do. They ask the right open questions to raise awareness and then listen attentively to the answers to allow the other person to come to their own powerful and unique solutions, the ones that are right for them and the situation. Coaches empower clients to take responsibility for their own lives and decisions.

If you translate this into leadership it means engaging with your staff with attention, taking the time to ask questions and listen to the answers; giving people an opportunity to develop awareness and take responsibility for their own work, including communicating sustainability to clients and colleagues – with the advantage that they will be much more invested in their jobs and, ultimately, more productive.

This is not an approach that works in a crisis as it takes time. In a crisis you *have to* be directive, and make fast, executive decisions instead. However, it would be the right approach on a day-to-day basis when you want a cohesive team that works harmoniously together like the Vienna Philharmonic Orchestra.

How to structure your conversations with your staff as a coach leader

Let me introduce you to a key tool in the coach leader toolbox: the TGROW model.[61] Coaches get taught this on day one of their coaching courses, but somehow the same doesn't happen in management. The TGROW model is used to guide coaches through their coaching conversations with clients with a structured path that allows the client to explain the topic (**T**) to focus on, clearly define a goal (**G**) for the session, explore the reality surrounding their challenge (**R**), work out some options (**O**) and think about a way forward (**W**). This tool will be

---

[61] Downey, M. (2003). *Effective Coaching: Lessons from the Coach's Coach.* Myles Downey has adapted the classic GROW (Goal, Reality, Options, Way Forward) coaching model by John Whitmore (*Coaching for Performance*, 1988) widely used to structure coaching conversations, by adding the T (Topic), which allows to differentiate between the bigger picture and the specific goal of the coaching conversation.

helpful for any conversation you have with your staff, but specifically in this case, to support your staff to have impactful conversations about sustainability.

I'll use a fictional scenario to walk you through it.

Topic: understand the context

Imagine you are the manager of a graduate consultant, Reese, who is new to her role in your sustainability firm and has so far only shadowed senior members of the team in meetings. She asks to see you and looks quite nervous. A first question you can ask her to understand the context could be: *What is the challenge/problem you are facing?*

Reese replies that next week she needs to have her first meeting on her own with a new client and she doesn't know where to start. She is technically brilliant but feels she can't speak articulately in meetings.

Goal: establish the goal they want to achieve

Establishing the goal of a meeting at the start of it is not something we do enough, but this is the reason why we attend so many useless meetings. Ensuring your staff has a clear idea of the purpose and objectives of the meetings they attend will maximize their productivity. So, now that the challenge is clear, you can start exploring what is the end goal of today's conversation.

Reese replies that she would like to work out how to overcome her fear, and was wondering whether you can help with some suggestions.

However, there is also another potential goal you can encourage Reese to think about, i.e. the result she'd like to achieve at the end of the meeting with the new client.

You might be tempted to tell your staff the reason why they are meeting the client but this is where you need to allow them to develop their own level of awareness and responsibility, and make their own choices with your guidance when needed, of course.

Reese says that she is not sure, perhaps to convince the client to adopt your company's new carbon calculator?

Although this is a sensible goal, and shows she has thought about the business opportunity, you might ask her how she came to this conclusion. Perhaps she did some research before meeting the client, so she knows this is definitely what they need? Or did she have an initial exchange with them?

Reese replies that she just thought that's what everyone in the company needs to do.

Asking questions instead of giving for granted that your staff know what to do is key to using a coaching approach in management. This approach allows you to uncover risks and opportunities.

In this case, Reese's goal was a projection of what she had witnessed in previous meetings – she didn't ask herself what would have been useful to discuss or discover at that initial meeting. And that's understandable: as a graduate consultant she'd not be expected to have a complete and mature view of the full process yet. So, you encourage her to think about what would be the best thing to do in a first meeting with anyone. She replies: *To get to know them.*

You explore how to do that with Reese, talking about good questions to ask to build rapport, then continue:

> *Since this will be your first meeting with your client, is there anything that you'd want to find out about them beforehand, so that you can help them address their challenges quicker and more accurately?*

> *Or are there any important questions you might want to ask them to understand their needs and wants before we suggest a specific solution?*

Hopefully, you can see here that by asking the right open questions and listening to the answers, you can uncover potential issues and guide your staff to become more aware of the best path to follow.

Reality: explore your staff's perspective

Question to ask: *What do you find specifically challenging in this upcoming client meeting?*

Here your staff might share their worries about the conversation or this specific client. Reese says that she finds it nerve-wracking to speak in front of a room full of executives when she is "just" a graduate consultant.

This is where deploying your emotional intelligence will help step into the other person's shoes, allowing you not to judge them or dismiss their concerns and support them in their professional journey instead. After all, you had been there, young and inexperienced, and it felt quite intimidating.[62]

Options: what can your staff do to address the issue?

Question to ask: *What are your options to overcome your challenge?*

This is where, with your support, your staff can start thinking options through to make the meeting effective and to reach the goals you have established at the start.

If they can't think of anything, you can use your active listening skills here to reflect on what they said earlier, perhaps you caught some words they used that can raise their self-awareness and empower them to move forward:

> *Reese, you said you want to have a successful meeting but feel unable to speak in front of senior executives. However, you did brilliantly at your interview for this position in front of our full C-suite, what can you learn from that experience that you can use in client meetings?*

If they feel really stuck, you might have some suggestions to offer them that have worked for you in the past – and this is where your personal

---

[62] *Empathic leadership* has been a popular expression for a few years now. Yet, in everyday office life, there are plenty of examples of leaders lacking empathy – whether because it just doesn't come natural to them, or because they are under pressure and cannot spare the time or headspace to think about how others feel. If you find yourself in this situation but want to embrace empathy, take the suggestion of Positive Intelligence's coach Shirzad Chamine (*Positive Intelligence: Why Only 20% of Teams and Individuals Achieve Their True Potential and How You Can Achieve Yours*, 2012) and imagine the person in front of you as their five-year old selves: it is easier to be empathic to a child than to an adult. This is a wonderful exercise to do on yourself too: just grab a childhood picture in which you are happy and "in your element", whether that's playing your favourite game or out in Nature, and try and spot your true essence. Then contemplate how that true essence is still in you – and how worthy of love and compassion you are, without needing to do or demonstrate anything to anybody.

experience can be a valuable mentoring tool for your staff's benefit ("Do you know what I always do before meetings to gain clarity? I jot down three key outcomes I want before I enter the meeting" or "I make sure I go for a brisk walk before important meetings to clear my head and take three deep breaths to recharge my brain"). Or you might suggest some resources (including this book!) that can be helpful to progress their thinking, a training course or coaching programme.

However, always offer advice lightly and only when asked since not every technique and strategy that worked for you will work for others. We too often offer unsolicited advice when others just need someone to listen to them.

Wrap up/will: summarize the conversation and commit to the next step

Questions to ask: *What are the next steps? What extra support do you need from this point onwards?*

You can ask your staff to summarize the conversation and share their next steps. This helps with accountability – your staff are saying out loud what they will do and this increases the chances they will actually take those steps – and to ensure you are all on the same page.

Reese says she will follow the process to have the powerful sustainability conversations shared in this book; then she will ground herself with a lunchtime run in the park before the meeting; finally, she will write down what went well and what can be improved for the next meeting, and reconvene with you to see whether she feels she needs extra support.

Key takeaways to shift mindsets in sustainability communication

Let's sum up what we looked at in Part 2: to successfully communicate sustainability, you, as a sustainability leader, will need to focus on shifting mindsets. Providing information and sharing data is the first step to raise awareness but it will not get others to act unless you approach your sustainability conversations differently. Here's how you can do it effectively, whether you are in a one-to-one conversation or presenting to a large audience.

Start by shifting your own mindset to be an effective communicator and develop resilience.

- Recognize what's going on in your own brain and its instinctive (lizard), emotional (mouse), and rational (human) responses. Pause when necessary to stop reacting instinctively and to allow your rational brain to respond calmly and wisely.

- To manage your mindset in challenging meetings, practise self-awareness and emotional control. If a discussion provokes a strong reaction, use deep breathing and sensory-focused techniques to regain clarity.

- Reframe issues to focus on problems, not people.

- Instead of pushing your ideas, seek to build rapport and common ground to co-create more fitting solutions.

- Regularly address your basic needs to maintain physical and mental wellbeing, enabling you to contribute effectively to sustainability efforts over the long term.

Spend time understanding your audience. Get to know the needs and motivations of your audience. You can use the DISC model (*Dominant, Influential, Steady* and *Compliant*) to gauge your audience's main personality traits and tailor your message and communication approach to resonate with their values, communication preferences and concerns.

Simplify your language. Avoid jargon and use clear, straightforward language.

Practise emotional intelligence. Communication is like a dance; you need to understand and anticipate others' moves. Listen attentively, pay close attention to your audience's reactions and be flexible in your approach.

Adopt a coaching leadership style. Empower your team to become good communicators by using a coach-like approach. The TGROW model (*Topic, Goal, Reality, Options, Way forward*) can help you to structure your conversations and guide your team effectively to influence others.

Utilize storytelling. Rethink your case studies and make sustainability relatable by transforming them into compelling stories including narrative, data and visuals.

By incorporating these strategies, you can shift mindsets and communicate sustainability in a way that inspires action and drives meaningful change. We will go into more detail on how to build meaningful and transformative sustainability conversations in Part 3.

Part 3
The Good
Communicator
framework

Figure 7 *Communicating sustainability is a journey!*

Introducing the Good Communicator framework

Imagine you borrowed a small, first-generation electric vehicle from a friend to take a journey across counties to an important conference that cannot be reached by public transport. The journey is short of 100 miles, so you think you can make it easily with a full battery. You pick up a client on the way to the destination and share the journey with them. They have to speak at the conference and you are going as a delegate.

They are not so keen (they secretly think you will both end up pushing the car on the motorway), but agreed, reluctantly, to share the journey. Both of you need to reach the conference location in time for their speech tomorrow. You have booked a hotel there for tonight. Now you have an hour or so to kill on the journey with this person you don't know well. So, you initiate a conversation, since you have nothing better to do.

You already know they are from a different country and moved here when they were young. This is an opportunity to ask a *deep question*[63] that, very quickly, will open up opportunities to get to know this person a little better. Instead of what people have been saying to me for the 20 years plus I lived in the UK (*What are you doing here?! Italy has much better food/weather!*) to which, in general, I smile politely and move on, you ask: *What do you miss the most about your country?*

---

[63] Deep questions are open questions that go deeper and touch on feelings, as we will see in Step 1 of the Good Communicator framework.

A few minutes into the journey and a conversation that has now quickly expanded to the state of the Planet and the future of our children, you realize that the available mileage range on the car dashboard is not reliable. Driving on the motorway is consuming a lot more battery than you expected. It's getting late and you need to think through some options with your client about what to do next. Stop at the next motorway services to recharge? Leave the car in the middle of the motorway and hitchhike a ride? Your client tells you of a nice little hotel close to the next motorway exit, which also has some EV charging points. Together you decide that the wisest thing to do is to stop at that hotel – which is closer than the services – and stay the night. Better not to risk having to hitchhike.

The seemingly small talk you had at the beginning of the journey, together with the deep question you asked, have managed to build rapid rapport between you and your client, so much so that you both felt comfortable sharing your views and quickly agreed on a solution that had a positive outcome for both of you. If you didn't ask those questions, your client would have probably jumped on their phones to check their emails or make some phone calls, leaving the decisions to you. You are notorious for having no patience, so you would have attempted the drive to the next services, ending up in a breakdown on the motorway.

Instead, you and your client analysed the current reality and worked together to find the best solution in the circumstances you were in. The day after, refreshed after a lovely breakfast, shower and a full car battery, you set off to the conference, which you reach in good time for the morning sessions. Your client is happy. You are happy. You have both reached your destination, even though you had different goals once there.

You didn't impose your views. You co-created with your client, and the end result was much better than it would have been had you decided for both of you.

This is exactly what I'm inviting you to do from now on, in any projects you'll encounter, and every conversation you will have when it comes to sustainability: **reframe it as a journey you will take together with others, even if they are reluctant to start with**.

Figure 8 The Good Communicator framework[64]

---

[64] I have introduced the TGROW coaching model in Part 2. The Good Communicator model is inspired by it but with the difference that here you are not enabling someone else's thinking: you are co-creating with others, which means you have to analyse the reality from various perspectives, and establish goals and think creatively about the solutions together. *Steps 4: Busting Barriers* and *5: Commitment and Way Forward*, cover techniques for you to ease the process and ensure the goals established together with your audience are reached, and the co-creation process is successful.

The Good Communicator framework, explained in detail in this part of the book, starts with getting to know each other and establishing quick rapport so that you have your audience's trust, any solution is perfectly tailored to their needs, and addresses their challenges and goal aspirations. But you have goals too (including considering the Planet's perspective) and you need to make sure the result is a success for you as well. You need to take a good look at the reality and work with the other person to understand how to reach those goals in the best possible way. You might find that there are obstacles along the way, but imposing your views or trying to fit any old solution in the name of sustainability will not generate positive or long-lasting results. It can also have implications for the relationship you have with the other person as they will feel threatened by your behaviour. Co-creating the solutions and analysing the wider implications together before agreeing on a way forward is a much more fitting and creative approach for everybody involved.

This framework is particularly relevant when you want to influence others to adopt sustainability and change the way they think about it, and you have had time to prepare, e.g. board and client meetings, strategic annual reviews, community engagement workshops, training courses, client pitches, etc. However, you will benefit from it even in casual conversations. The principles are the same, but you might have less of a chance to follow the steps and prepare as these conversations might happen impromptu. If, however, you use this method regularly, the gist of it will become ingrained in you and you will be able to use it without much thinking in those less formal situations as well.

From unprepared to unstoppable: my journey with the Good Communicator framework

Ben G is the Head of Sustainability of a FTSE250 manufacturing company.

Adopting the Good Communicator framework in my day-to-day working life has been a journey of self-discovery. I wasn't expecting that, but the biggest lesson learned in this process has been to be able to detect the negative narrative and the damning voice in my head screaming at me: "DO NOT FEEL, DO NOT THINK". That voice previously meant I would go blindly into meetings with little prior preparation (although, incidentally, I had an objective to do my work more intentionally this year).

I looked at the Good Communicator framework's steps and asked myself how they would best apply to an in house sustainability person.

Essentially, they fulfil the needs of what I now call the Six Ps (Prior Preparation Prevents Pitifully Poor Performance). Actively thinking about my goals for a meeting and the personalities of attendees has allowed me to tailor my message in a way that speaks to those personalities.

This has meant that in the past few weeks I have overcome a number of hurdles and situations that had been difficult to progress, like Annual Report discussions, an ESG strategy Launch and ESG strategy Objectives. Grounding myself for a few minutes before a meeting has helped, mostly when combined with proper preparation, as it allows me a moment to centre myself and remember my prep.

I have noticed that applying these techniques with some good time management techniques (I use time blocking at the beginning of every day to plan, then on a Friday to plan for the following week; I also block out 15 minutes before and after every meeting in my calendar to make sure I am ready and that I write my reflections and action points at the end) has resulted in me speaking more confidently, and delegating much more as I am winning discussions and influencing others more effectively.

My workload is getting lighter and things are progressing.

The Good Communicator framework is enabling our journey of embedding sustainability into the DNA of the business by making other departments (other than the core sustainability team) take ownership over it.

Step 1: Building rapport and exploring the reality

Imagine that you, like test pilot Tuck Pendleton in the 1987 movie *Innerspace*, have been injected into your client's body (stay with me here… please). If you have watched this classic film, you'll know what I'm talking about. If not, just imagine you are about to take a voyage inside your client. The mission involves finding the answer to the biggest mystery: *What does your client think?*

And not just that. We want to discover more than just what's in their brains but also what's in their hearts. Every conversation is a negotiation, and every negotiation is conducted and concluded at an emotional level, deeply connected with the values and beliefs of each party. Therefore, we want to understand what the other person is interested in, what they believe in and what they value.

And here I'm not just talking about their company – that's an element of it – but about their *personal* preferences. Remember, every single negotiation is done between people, not companies. You want to make sure they buy into solutions that can change their mindset and business future while having a positive impact on the Planet, not pushing your ideas no matter what.

So, it is worth spending time understanding the person who is leading the negotiation from the other side. And because you don't have a miniaturized submersible pod to do that, you need to communicate with them.

Why building rapport is important

Building rapport with the people you want to talk to about sustainability is not just important, it is fundamental and it is *the* skill you will need to practise the most. The advantages are numerous, as follows.

- Science has demonstrated that people become *more likeable and trustworthy* when they are good communicators, i.e. when they show a genuine interest in others, ask them questions and listen attentively to the answers.[65]

- This means that your collaboration will be more fruitful and you'll have a better chance to influence others to *change behaviours* when needed.

- You will better understand their *needs and wants*, and whether there are any discrepancies between the two, which will avoid misunderstandings and expensive mistakes.

- Because the communication channels will be more open, you'll be able to ask more *specific* and *relevant questions* and get more *thorough answers*.

- In turn, this will allow you to spot *risks* and *opportunities* you might not discover otherwise.

Since we started switching most of our meetings from in-person to virtual from the COVID-19 pandemic onwards, we have become contemporary centaurs: half pyjamas, half blazers. We can conveniently jump from call to call without wasting time tidying up rooms after meetings. However, we have lost a fundamental part of what makes us human: small talk. The water-cooler moments. The life-sharing snippets that differentiate us from super-efficient AI – without considering the natural time needed to process how our meetings go and any impressions and ideas that come out from our conversations.

We often go straight into the meeting's agenda. Somehow it feels inappropriate and a waste of time to ask about people's families on a work video call.

---

[65] Sievers, B. et al. (2020). How consensus-building conversation changes our minds and aligns our brains, *PsyArXiv*, 12 July 2020.

As a consequence, we suffer from "Zoom fatigue"[66] caused by always looking at each other in the eyes, moving around less, having to be always on, showing others that we are following with physical gestures like thumbs up and clapping hands. I'd add it also dehumanizes our business relationships, with long-term consequences on the success of the projects we work on and, ultimately, our ability to get others on board with our ideas.

Years ago, I visited Qatar for the first time on a work trip. It surprised me that all meetings always started with fairly lengthy small talk about the attendees' travels, family, health even: anything but business. I then learned that, in the UAE (United Arab Emirates), trust and respect fostered through proper etiquette are paramount and these are best built through getting to know each other personally via small talk in face-to-face meetings.[67]

In fact, trust underpins *every* exchange we have in society, from trusting the pilot of your plane to fly you safely to your destination, to trusting your doctor to give you the right diagnosis and treatment, to trusting authorities to keep society operating peacefully.[68]

Creating rapport and trust with others quickly (whether via video calls or in person) is a key skill to master to build those bridges that will make you a good communicator, someone who catalyses other people's attention and creates the conditions to build a sustainable world with them.

The matching principle

Isn't it great when we "click" with someone? We feel energized, we finish each other's sentences, and we laugh and cry together. But how come we connect so deeply with some people and not at all with others?

Numerous studies have shown that when we connect with someone effectively our brains and even our bodies become alike and we become,

[66] Bailenson, J. N. (2021). Nonverbal overload: A theoretical argument for the causes of Zoom fatigue. *Technology, Mind, and Behavior*, 2(1).

[67] Visit Dubai – Official Tourism Board in Dubai (n.d.). www.visitdubai.com/

[68] Frei, F. X. and Morriss, A. (May–June 2020). Everything starts with trust. *Harvard Business Review*. https://hbr.org/2020/05/begin-with-trust

as neuroscientists put it, *neurally entrained*.[69] Our neurons synchronize like migrating birds.

Some of us are natural-born "supercommunicators" as journalist and author Charles Duhigg defines them.[70] Supercommunicators tend to be entrusted with power, have larger-than-average social networks, and are asked for advice more often. Interestingly, they are not the dominant leaders who steal the scene and talk about themselves and their opinions *ad nauseam*. Instead, they gently lead others *by asking more questions* (up to 20 times more!), mirror other people's emotions, and encourage them to listen to each other.

In research groups in which there was a "supercommunicator", people tended to agree with them more easily.[71] This means that when you manage to connect with others and your brains' wavelengths match, you are not only trusted more but you become more likeable and people listen to what you say. But how can you build rapport *if you are not* a natural-born supercommunicator?

How to build rapid rapport with people: networking and first encounters

Ever been at a networking event in which you didn't know anyone?

For those of us who are not naturally inclined to social interactions, this is a nightmare scenario. Where do you even start? Do you barge into a group that is already in a flurry of conversations? Do you pick another person looking lost like you by the coffee machine and ask them about the weather? Do you just grab a croissant and pretend to look at your phone?

After years of networking, I realized how challenging it can be to network in a way that feels "natural" and that builds genuine rapport with total strangers.

---

[69] Lakatos, P., Gross, J., and Thut, G. (2019). A new unifying account of the roles of neuronal entrainment. *Current Biology*, 29(18), R890–R905; Menenti, L., Pickering, M. J. and Garrod, S. C. (June 2012). Toward a neural basis of interactive alignment in conversation. *Frontiers in Human Neuroscience*. Vol. 6. Article 185.

[70] Duhigg, C. (2024). *Supercommunicators: How to Unlock the Secret Language of Connection.*

[71] Sievers, B. et al. (2020). How consensus-building conversation changes our minds and aligns our brains, PsyArXiv, 12 July 2020.

I used to be the one in a corner, preferring to cuddle a glass of red and stare at the paintings on the wall than interacting with strangers. But it is possible to change. Over the years I learned that networking, especially in sustainability, is an important, even necessary, thing we have to do.

Meeting others and co-creating is the *only* way forward to make this world a more just and liveable place... But, boy, how awkward it can be.

So here are three fictional characters you might find at networking events who showcase some potential networking challenges when meeting people for the first time.

Sam

Sam is friendly and shakes your hand firmly. He smiles and welcomes you. Lovely start. But when you ask him what he does, he starts to tell you all about his great job, his industry, the book he wrote... Sam doesn't say uninteresting things, he just doesn't ask you any questions. He's an accomplished, very self-assured professional but his networking style is more like lecturing, and his conversation style is a monologue, not a dialogue.

Sally

Sally doesn't smile and doesn't show any enthusiasm when meeting you. She says she owns a zero-waste shop nearby and since you are genuinely interested in that, you ask about the location. She answers briefly then excuses herself and walks off without asking any questions to you. You smell your armpits and ask yourself if perhaps you stink...

Steve

Steve is a lovely man, obviously 100% committed to sustainability and very active in various community initiatives. But Steve whispers. You cannot hear him when he speaks just three feet away from you. You try to guess what he's saying amid the noise around you, then just pretend you heard and nod.

Can you see a pattern? None of these great people doing great things in sustainability showed an interest in the person in front of them. None of them stepped into your shoes or wondered how you felt or what you thought. But fear not, in situations like these, you can always try to make it better.

Whether you tend to be like one of those characters or you come across one, see whether you feel comfortable stepping into the other person's shoes. Show an interest. Smile. Ask questions as well as talking about yourself. Is there something that picked your interest in the other person or what they said? Can you ask them more about it? Is your tone of voice adequate to the situation, or can you ask the other person to move somewhere a little quieter so that you can hear each other without straining?

Networking events – and any time you meet someone for the first time – should be reframed as business dates. You should not be there to sell your services or to boast about your wonderful career, but to get to know people. Especially in sustainability, these connections can be a long shot but they are fundamental to building community and working together towards a better future.

After many years of awkward networking events, I have honed my technique, which – in addition to avoiding the pitfalls embodied by Sam, Sally and Steve – you can use any time you need to create rapid rapport with someone you don't know, like a new client at the start of your professional relationship.

Before the event, I try to learn more about who is going to be there. Is there a guest list that I can access? Do I know who's joining the event? If so, who do I really want to speak to?

If I know who will be there and I identify a couple of people I want to speak to, this becomes my goal for that event. I'll check their LinkedIn profile or website to see whether I can spot something interesting to ask them about or anything we have in common (a connection, a past work experience or an interest).

This might not work entirely at an online networking event, when you can be randomly put in breakout rooms with people you don't know. My take on those is that the reason you join them is usually that you want to expand your network. So especially in these events, let serendipity take its course and get to know people first and foremost, without agenda. Just listen to what they have to say. Then you can use the techniques that follow when it comes to introducing yourself, which are valid for in person and online events alike.

During the event, most people will introduce themselves with their name and profession. But unless you are looking after gorillas in a Ugandan sanctuary or are a scientist working on a filter to refract solar radiation to space to limit global warming, people may not be that interested in your job and might not ask any questions that can spark a conversation.

While it's important to share who you are and what you do, especially in a business context, how about adding something *personal* about your job or your interest in sustainability? Something that can stimulate curiosity in the other person?

After I say my name, I have learned to say that I support sustainability professionals to amplify their impact with the ultimate goal of making sustainability a no-brainer for everyone. The question that usually follows is: *How do you do THAT?* Only then do I say that I am a coach and a trainer and, if asked, I share my working ethos: helping people advance their careers in sustainability, and companies to work better together so that they can make a difference. Can you see how I include my passion and vision for sustainability in my *social pitch*? I'm sharing not only *facts* but also the way *I feel* about this topic.

Now, depending on what you are sharing, it can feel pretty vulnerable. At first, I thought it was too cheesy and I felt awkward – after all, I was doing something completely different from the rest of the room. However, the more I rehearsed and tried it in networking situations, the more I had a positive response, the more confident I felt. People generally feel intrigued and ask further questions or share their own passion for sustainability, which starts to align our views and builds up that connection.

Sometimes you might want to let other people go first. Chances are they will introduce themselves in the usual way (name and profession) to which you can respond by asking something about a fact you have learned about them beforehand or the event you are attending. Another idea is to try to find a shared experience with them – perhaps their country of origin or a qualification. And this can be followed by a *deep question*.

A **deep question** is an open question that deviates from facts and practicality (like your job title) and goes into how people *feel* about their lives. It touches on values and beliefs which, if they resonate, makes the connection between people immediate. You could ask for instance:

> *How did you decide to become what you are now?*

Or if you know their background, for instance the university they went to, you could say:

> *Forgive me, but I stalked you on LinkedIn before this event, and I noticed you went to Oxford Brookes University. I did my Master's there, and loved the passion tutors had. What was your experience like?*

This would be a light-hearted way to explore their views on life while finding common ground.

Heroes vs. enemies

When we approach a conversation ready to fight with our gloves on, we subconsciously imply the other person is our enemy.

We are there to fight them as if they were a foreign land to conquer, no better than the Europeans did when they landed in 1492 on the East Coast of America, stubbornly convinced they reached India, and started a systematic process of subduing and exterminating the American Indigenous populations.

Imagine if, instead of oppressing them by imposing their own culture, the Europeans became *truly curious* about these Indigenous populations. Perhaps they would have learned how they believed that humans are part of Nature instead of its masters, and brought back some of that wisdom to Europe.[72] Would we have had this consumeristic outlook on life now? Would things have been different because working with Nature instead of exploiting it would have been the norm?

If history can teach us something, it is that imposing our views on others is never a good thing long term. That's why I'm so against the common argument many sustainability professionals adopt to convince their clients: *You have to do it because it's a legal obligation.* Sure, that could be *one* driver. But it cannot be the only motivator. Because the minute that specific project is over, that client will avoid sustainability if they can.

So, if the person we are speaking to is not our enemy to be defeated and overcome, who are they? The *hero*, of course!

I know I'm asking you A LOT: to consider someone you probably dislike as the hero of the situation. But many successful serial entrepreneurs, from Richard Branson to Daniel Priestly, will tell you that being in business is essentially about helping others and making a difference in their lives. Even if you don't have a business of your own at the moment, you are *in* business. And your mission must be about helping others.

Changing perspective sometimes helps.

So, imagine you have landed on the Moon. What you see from there is our gorgeous little blue marble, the Earth, floating in the dark universe. Fashion, social media, priceless artworks, sports cars, presidents and

---

[72] Lee, G. (1994). Did early Native Americans live in harmony with nature? *Washington Post*, December 4; Lewis, D. R. (1995). Native Americans and the environment: A survey of twentieth-century issues, *American Indian Quarterly*, 19(3), 423-450; Vanorio, A. (2020). *What Native Americans Teach Us About Sustainability*. www.foxrunenvironmentaleducationcenter.org/ecopsychology/2020/6/8/what-native-americans-teach-us-about-sustainability

slums, arguing over who took the rubbish out last, even illnesses and conflicts... they are all there, but so tiny you can't even see them.

And I doubt you'd even think about them while you are speechless before the beauty of the sight you are so lucky to witness – unless you want to take a selfie to post on your Instagram account...

Once you see how small everything is, compared to the vastness of the universe, you also realize that that's all we've got. That little blue marble is our home and the most precious thing we have. Your nice clients are there too, as well as your horrible clients, and your bosses. They are all on the same mothership as yours. And to save it from collapse, we have to work together and get past the pettiness generated by our egos.

In 1936, Dale Carnegie published the world-famous *How to Win Friends and Influence People*. The sixth principle of this classic book is: *Make the other person feel important – and do it sincerely*. Carnegie recalls paying a compliment to the cashier at the post office about his gorgeous hair for no reason other than having done something for that person without expecting a return. He writes:

> If we are so contemptibly selfish that we can't radiate a little happiness and pass on a bit of honest appreciation without trying to get something out of the other person in return – if our souls are no bigger than sour crab apples, we shall meet with the failure we so richly deserve.

Most people crave recognition. If you strive to find something you honestly admire about the other person without any hidden agenda but to create that bond that will make you and the other person happier when you work together or just make each other's day, you'll see your life – and your power to influence others – transform dramatically as a side effect.

Carnegie quotes Benjamin Disraeli, a late XIX-century British statesman: "Talk to people about themselves and they will listen for hours." It can be as simple as talking about people's interests when meeting them. Learn *with curiosity* what they like and enjoy, and talk about it.

Who is *really* involved in this conversation? The value of stakeholder mapping

Imagine that a new client who owns a supermarket chain tells you they want a new fleet of electric vehicles to cut their logistics-related emissions. When you hold the first meeting with them you might be speaking with one person but, behind them, there will be a full board of directors as well as their investors, the community that surrounds them, their clients…

If you are dealing with a large corporation in which your reference point is one of the directors, many other people will need to be involved, informed and consulted before any decision is taken. Of course, if you are dealing with a small enterprise, things might be easier as there might be just one or two decision-makers. However, for the outcomes of a project to be truly sustainable, you'll need to consider all the stakeholders involved nevertheless, even (and especially!) the silent ones.

No business is built in a silo; not even sole traders work completely on their own. Therefore it's worth considering as a minimum the following stakeholders and how they are going to be affected by, or affect, the project (or even just the conversation you are having):

- top management

- shareholders/investors/donors

- staff

- suppliers

- partners

- customers

- local and national government

- communities

- media

- the Planet (this could be local biodiversity, soil, atmosphere and so on).

Inviting Nature to the decision table

David S is the Director of a non-for-profit enterprise using Nature-based solutions to enhance biodiversity and capture carbon.

If I had a magic wand I would make it business-as-usual to have Nature at the boardroom table as a Stakeholder – rather than being an Any Other Business (AOB). Then before any question is answered and any decision taken, I would ask: *Can Nature provide any answers?*

The good news is, you don't have to convince *everybody* within a company that sustainability is the way forward! You just need to be strategic about who you focus your energy and time on.

Consider your audience and plot them into a chart of *Power vs. Interest* (see Figure 9).

Figure 9 Power vs. Interest stakeholder map

- Who is *powerful* and therefore influential enough and has an *interest* in sustainability? If you are dealing with someone like that you have just won the jackpot! They will be your *promoters*, helping you champion your ideas within the company and making your life a lot easier. In the scenario of the supermarket wanting to get new electric vehicles not every director will be interested in this project. Your promoters could be the Head of Sustainability and the HR Director, who have in the past championed sustainability in the company. They can help you get traction with their peers. Just like in politics, your efforts should be focused on those who are already interested and see the value in what you are offering and those who are neutral about it (the swing voters) and can be convinced by well-constructed arguments and facts, especially those with influencing powers within the company.

- If there are, on the other hand, people who are powerful and deadly against your ideas (*latents*) you might want to get someone with power and influence to work on them.

- Don't forget to involve (and at the very least consider, like in the case of Nature) the highly interested stakeholders even when they haven't got much power (*defenders*), not only because it's the right thing to do but also because they can support you in other ways: for instance, by championing your ideas with others and creating a grassroots movement, like local communities, who will benefit from cleaner air, or staff champions, who can support your sustainability efforts inside the company. People are more likely to be swayed by their own peers whom they already know and trust than by outsiders.

Transforming team dynamics towards company-wide sustainable change

Ben G, who we met earlier in Part 3, is the Head of Sustainability for a FTSE250 manufacturing company.

Our sustainability team's objective is to influence our own colleagues to make their standard operations more sustainable. A major challenge we had before adopting the Good

Communicator framework was that our sustainability team went from two to nine people in the space of three months, which meant refocusing and managing the diverse personalities and dynamics of a very new team.

Initially, we struggled also with direction due to the sustainability topic's broad and poorly defined nature. We had to punch above our weight to influence far more senior colleagues to change strategy and find resources, when they were not completely on board.

Using the DISC assessment helped alleviate team tensions as we started to better understand each other's communication styles, strengths and personalities. We learned to focus on what we can control and let go of everything else. We also carried out some stakeholder mapping to understand who we should focus our attention on. We started prioritizing tasks more effectively by becoming more realistic about our capabilities.

As a consequence of this work, we purposefully reduced the core sustainability team's size to six. The others have moved out of the sustainability team and now sit in the business functions that have the biggest challenges and solutions: we realized we needed our sustainability staff to closely support the development of business function-led solutions.

This move allowed the core team to focus more on selling and communicating sustainability rather than providing technical support.

We now have at least one sustainability champion in each division that we directly deal with and who can promote sustainability internally with the other key stakeholders.

This shift led to broader acceptance of sustainability initiatives across the company, so much so that we have just had our second round of strategy, which for the first time has been developed by everybody in the senior management team as a massive co-creation exercise.

We successfully influenced senior management and strategy, embedding sustainability objectives within product groups and sales regions, and leading to impactful changes such as each product group now measuring their carbon footprints and adjusting business strategies accordingly.

Focusing on building rapport within the team and with the colleagues outside our team and on being strategic about which key stakeholders to influence and how, has transformed the way sustainability is now perceived and implemented company-wide.

The importance of preparation

Raise your hand if, at least once, you went into a meeting without having a specific idea of why you were there. Yep, guilty as charged.

We have all done it: rushing from one meeting to another, we sometimes fail to prepare, so we sit down and hope that someone else will speak first so we can catch our breath and gather our thoughts.

In an ideal world, you have looked up the person(s) you are meeting beforehand and have had some initial conversations perhaps via email. You already have an idea of what the objective of the conversation will be, and of your audience's key issues.

However, if you really haven't got the time to do any prep before the meeting, aim at building rapport rapidly (as explained earlier in this step) by paying as much attention as possible to the people you meet during the meeting and asking the right questions to explore their perspective and to understand the context surrounding the project or the conversation.

This is essential to co-create some meaningful goals for your audience, the Planet and you.

Step 2: Goals

Step 1 was all about building rapport and establishing the reality of the situation. In Step 2 we will explore how to co-operatively establish goals with your audience.

Needs vs. wants

Right at the outset, it is helpful to set goals for your conversation and/or the wider project. The goals will need to reflect the needs of everyone involved, Planet included. So it's important to *start from the end*, as opposed to starting from where you are right now. Why?

Because if you start from the current reality, you might end up somewhere you don't want to: it is likely that the current reality wasn't created with ambitious sustainability goals in mind. Instead, if you start the process from the goals you all want to achieve from now on, this new destination will determine the steps to take, starting today, to get there.

In the supermarket chain scenario (see Step 1), if you start from the presumed end of buying a new fleet of EV vehicles, your client could end up spending a lot of time and money when there is no need, not to mention the environmental impact. Establishing that the end goal is actually a 50% reduction in carbon emissions[73] may make the route there look very different.

---

[73] What a client might not know is the difference between *performance targets* (in this case, carbon reduction) and *specific tech solutions* (the EVs). When setting long-term targets, you can explain that it's always best to have performance-related goals rather

For this reason, before setting goals for the conversation or a larger project that will stem from it, it's important to identify and differentiate between the other person's *needs* and *wants*.

They could be the same but they could also be very different things. And if you help the person you are dealing with to do what they want without questioning it, it might end up being not the best option for them, you or the Planet. For instance, in the example of the supermarket chain looking to cut their logistic-related emissions, they want a whole fleet of new EVs when what they might need at this stage is to rethink the logistics of their deliveries so that they save money, fuel and carbon with their existing fleet.

But how do you uncover the reality and, most importantly, what's best for them without imposing it or getting a rejection? You need to identify the root causes of the issues your client is dealing with, and create an environment for the project to thrive based on its connections with the past, current and future context, other people and organizations, and Nature (the silent stakeholder).

You will already have established your stakeholders and identified the key ones in the conversation. Now you will need to consider the views of each of these, what they need and want.

These principles are based on *systems thinking* which, if you are unfamiliar with it, means that we need to look at an issue as part of a wider system and at its relationship and connections with the other parts of the system, instead of as an isolated event.[74] Systems thinking is the ideal problem-solving framework to address sustainability since it consists of very complex, dynamic interconnections of issues affecting one another.

As human beings, we tend to rationalize and simplify the issues we deal with because it's easier to grasp them. But as we know, sustainability is a slippery fish and no issue has simply one solution without having a

---

than tech-related ones, as tech evolves rapidly and, in time, they might want to adopt a more efficient solution that reaches their performance targets quicker than EVs. Also, performance targets can be achieved by a *range* of solutions worth exploring, instead of picking a specific one because they have seen someone else adopting it.

[74] See Appendix B for a more detailed explanation of Systems Thinking in sustainability.

knock-on effect on other things. So, we have to embrace the complexity as much as possible.

How?

By becoming a badger. Digging deep into the issues. Asking questions. Being curious. Trying to determine the root causes of people's behaviours and their consequences. Questioning the status quo. Finding connections between different elements of the system you are looking at, both in time (what happened before and what will happen in the future if a specific decision is taken today) and space (think things at different scales and from different perspectives – the community, the soil and the air, other businesses).

Most people struggle to understand systems thinking and to apply it in real-life situations.

Taking it for granted that you don't want to spend years learning the theory of systems thinking, I'm offering here a practical approach that can do the trick for most projects: a series of targeted questions and perhaps a *causal loop* sketch[75] on the back of an envelope.

But the starting point is to think about the topic of this conversation (and perhaps the wider project) as part of a *system* as illustrated a little later, and about the connections between the elements and how whatever decisions come out of this conversation will affect the other elements.

For instance, in the supermarket chain that wants a new EV fleet scenario (*the system*), the interconnected elements that will be affected by or affect this change are as follows.

- **Internal stakeholders:** top management, staff, in particular drivers and those responsible for logistics.

- **External stakeholders:** the community around the supermarkets, local authorities, transport and environment authorities, other connected businesses (supply chain, local businesses), customers,

---

[75] We will look at how to draw a causal loop diagram in *Step 3: Co-creation*, and you can find the specific questions to ask to find any issue's root causes in *Appendix B: The Iceberg Model*.

media outlets, the heritage of the locations where the shops are located, etc.

- **Nature:** air, land, water and wildlife.

- **Any other PESTLE (Political, Environmental, Social, Technological, Legislative and Economic) factors**, e.g. any grants available to buy EVs, new technologies increasing the driving range of EVs or international anti-modern slavery laws that protect workers in countries where the minerals to build EV batteries are sourced.

A further step will be to understand how these elements are connected to each other and evolve over time. For instance, a government grant will make it economically viable for the supermarket chain to purchase a new EV fleet, which will make the air around their stores cleaner, in turn positively affecting the community around it.

However, the older vehicles will need to be scrapped, which will generate waste and potential harm to Nature if not disposed of correctly. Over time, there will be the issue of EV battery disposal, which new technological advancements might eventually address. And so on...

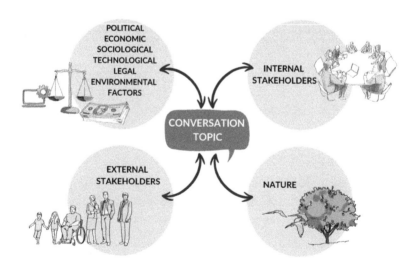

Figure 10 Systemic relationships between the topic of conversation and its influencing factors

Although no solution will ever be perfect, the "right" goals will have the power to have mostly positive effects on society, environment and economy while limiting (or better, reversing) negative impacts.

The best way to determine connections and identify your audience's needs is to ask questions about their *challenges*.

As we said earlier, needs and wants can be two very different things. What a person or company wants (e.g. a new EV fleet) might not be what they actually need (e.g. reduce their carbon emissions from transport by 50% with a combination of optimization strategies for their existing fleet).

Here is a list of potential questions to ask:

What's your biggest challenge?[76]

What do your colleagues see as their biggest challenge(s) in this area?

How do these challenges affect people (staff, community, supply chain)/ processes/the Planet/your company?

Are there any PESTLE factors that can positively or negatively affect the current situation? What about in the future?

It is plausible that, at this stage, your audience will not be completely aware of the full breadth of their challenges, but going through the context thoroughly will raise their awareness.

Marrying needs with wants

We have looked at establishing your audience's needs by asking about their challenges and understanding the context in as much depth as possible. But you need another step before you can firm up the goals for the conversation/project.

You need to explore what outcome your audience *wants*, and ask open questions to understand the underlying reasons: any misalignment with

---

[76] Note that often they will say money, but this might hide a fear of losing something else, like their reputation or their autonomy. Sometimes it will be the need to reach a new customer base, or remain relevant in the fast-paced marketplace. If in doubt, check whether any of the SCARF psychological issues are at play here – see Part 1.

what they actually need might have some negative impacts on Planet, People and Profit.

Some potential questions could be:

What do you want to accomplish?

What's the value of reaching this goal for you?

How does this fit into your company's vision and mission?

How on board are the people not in this meeting?

How will this goal affect all the other stakeholders (including Nature) involved?

And, most importantly to understand any gaps between needs and wants:

Why do you want (or not want) this specific solution?

In the supermarket chain example, it might emerge that one of the directors saw a competitor parading a shiny new fleet of electric vehicles and wanted to do the same (notice how there is some ego at play here… they probably wanted to personally look good and forward-thinking in front of their customers, competitors and bosses).

But their real need is to save money and carbon and new EVs would cause a logistic issue due to the average short range of their engines, without taking into account the capital costs of buying them.

Take it for granted that the average adult in a business context feels their status is in jeopardy if they show vulnerability or ignorance. As a consequence, they tend not to ask for further explanations if something is not clear. In this case, your client might be unaware of the spread of other potential solutions available to them from optimized delivery schedule and route adjustments to smaller vehicles for local deliveries to some second-hand EVs as opposed to a whole fleet to fuel-saving driving techniques: all potentially valid alternatives that depend on a number of variables, like their current emission baseline, target emissions, capital availability or top management commitment.

Only you as the expert will be able to work out what's the best technical solution for the specific situation, but you need them to provide information, company insight and a pair of fresh eyes. So, let's get down from the ivory tower and start working with people on the ground. The person in front of you might not have sustainability technical knowledge but they will know their business inside out.

You are the curator of the plethora of conflicting and confusing information about sustainability out there, and need to tailor them to your audience's needs. You know the solutions but don't know the context they can fit in (their business) as well as them.

That's why you need to work together with your audience to marry needs and wants to reach the perfect bespoke solution.

Project vs. strategic sustainability goals: how to persuade your audience to go for more

Now, troubles start when your goals are not in line with our audience's. It's as if you are speaking different languages in the same conversation and cannot understand each other – in fact, there is a misalignment of neural wavelengths.

As part of the research for this book, I spoke to many sustainability professionals to understand the approaches they take to convince others that sustainability is a good idea. *Every single person* I spoke to is animated by a strong desire to make the Planet better. They are often scared by the climate crisis and its consequences. They suffer from *solastalgia*, a form of distress experienced when the environment around an individual undergoes destructive change, threatening their sense of identity, belonging and emotional wellbeing.[77] This can induce *eco-anxiety* so they are moved by a sense of urgency to fix things. This concoction of emotions, from passion to frustration to depression to anger, can be reflected in the way sustainability professionals approach their audience's issues. Their strong emotions and values are the compass of the conversations. But, as explained earlier in this book, strong emotions have to be managed and

---

[77] Albrecht, G., Sartore, G. M., Connor, L., Higginbotham, N., Freeman, Ss, Kelly, B., Stain, H., Tonna, A., and Pollard, G. (2007). Solastalgia: The distress caused by environmental change. *Australasian Psychiatry*, 15(1): S95–98.

channelled to fuel our motivation to reach our goals, or else our lizard brain will kick off with unintended consequences.

This "knight in armour" approach has in itself a righteous flavour that immediately puts a barrier between the person who is speaking and their audience.

Bringing your own values to the boardroom without having done the work of shifting your mindset and developing your resilience first will become a barrier to your ability to connect with others and not only reach but even set the right goals. Additionally, when you use your values to pivot conversations and negotiations, you might find that your audience does not share the same values as you and that means a schism happening from the start.

Many sustainability professionals feel that selling is unethical. A passion for sustainability can come with an equally strong dislike of capitalism as the main culprit of the disaster we are in. As such, money is seen as a necessary evil in all negotiations, left at the end after all the ethical arguments have been pushed forward. But we need to take into account that even though our destination is the three Ps (but first People and Planet, then Profit), our audiences might want to focus entirely on Profit and consider the other two purely as means to this end.

Does that mean they are all bad people?

Not necessarily. But it can feel like it. Hence our need to, nervously, put our boxing gloves on and prepare for the fight. The result is that sustainability professionals who have not developed their resilience and communication strategy yet tend to succumb to their audience's will and go with their low-hanging-fruit goals: a tick-box exercise certification; after-thought photovoltaic panels on a roof; one "eco" t-shirt in a 52-piece collection; one sustainability officer when they'd need five; and the list continues.

They may stop trying to persuade their audience that sustainability is the *perfect solution* for them as soon as their audience brings up the classic objection: "We don't have the resources for it." So, one green-tinted solution becomes an easy way to comply with whatever short-term obligation the audience has and sustainability doesn't become embedded in their long-term strategies. The consequences are low impact, frustration, loss of faith in humanity. Because we are scared of the fight. We don't feel equipped for it. We don't have the right weapons. But do you know what? You don't need to fight.

Reframing the issue and cultivating a growth mindset

If you manage to separate the person from the issue and focus on the latter as the problem to be solved, it will be a lot easier to agree on common goals that will satisfy everyone involved. Because we are not negatively charging the conversation towards a fight and making it personal: we are not trying to "fix" someone, but an issue.

For this reason, it's important not to imply other people are wrong and you are right, triggering their defences. If anything, *you'll want* to work with the other person to address the issue, because you value their opinion and experience. You couldn't do it without them. They are key to finding that perfect triple-win solution. What you need to imply is that you are here *to help* your audience address an issue they are dealing with, not to change their mind, with the perfect solution (which happens to be a sustainable solution).

Ever since starting my sustainability journey, I thought sustainability is the *common sense* and the *responsible* thing to do. In most situations in life and business, why wouldn't you want a solution that considers everyone's rights and needs, encourages social justice, and doesn't harm the environment? Who would want to run an irresponsible business? A welcome consequence of getting others to see the common sense and responsible side of sustainability is that they will, during this process, perhaps change their mind.

What if people don't see it this way and they think sustainability is a nice addition rather than a necessity? How about using the *Power of Yet?*

A few years ago, Carol Dweck delivered a powerful TEDx Talk[78] in which she talked about the value of a simple mindset shift that supports

---

[78] Dweck, C. (2014). *The power of believing that you can improve* [Video]. TED Talks. www.ted.com/talks/carol_dweck_the_power_of_believing_that_you_can_improve

motivation, resilience and continuous development in children. But this is something that we can embrace as adults too. Our *negativity bias*, and repeated "failures" when it comes to selling sustainability to others might have calcified the belief that we are incapable of communicating sustainability effectively. Or to throw the baby out with the bathwater and believe that all clients/board members care only about money. This is an example of a fixed mindset that will lower your confidence and be a self-fulfilling prophecy in which you will not be able to persuade anyone to adopt sustainability.

Thinking that you haven't worked out how to handle this specific issue *yet* is much more powerful and opens up more possibilities than ruminating over your failure to convince someone to adopt sustainability.

I'm suggesting that you forget about changing someone's mind (which is very hard) and instead work on a process to address the issue *with* them.

If this doesn't happen at the first meeting, tell yourself that you haven't found the right approach *yet*. This implies that you will, one day. Even if today is not that day.

Your mission in this journey is to ensure your audience sees the full value of a sustainable outcome, even if they currently want Profit, and not because you want to make them tree-huggers like you, but because the solutions you are proposing are the most sensible ones for a *responsible* business like theirs.

Persistence in action: engaging team members in sustainability

Amy D is a built environment sustainability consultant.

It's important to keep going, keep smiling, and not lose hope of reaching out to someone.

I worked with a contractor firm where a team member used to tut at everything I said in meetings, but as soon as we started discussing ecology issues he was suddenly very engaged and asking if we could do more. It could have been that he really didn't engage with energy and carbon while, unbeknown to me, ecology was his passion. Had I given up immediately and convinced myself that I wasn't able to communicate sustainability, I wouldn't have built any rapport with this person and, as a consequence, pushed sustainability further in the project.

The business case for sustainability

Your clients might have approached you because sustainability is a funding or permit condition in their project. They might want to build a new building or launch a new clothing line that appeals to the younger generations. Perhaps your directors' board wants to appeal to a wider customer base, so they asked you to draft a Diversity and Inclusivity policy.

That's their destination, while the sustainability element is only a means to an end. For you, sustainability is *the* destination. You will have the health of the Planet and People at your heart. But let's not forget, a person cannot survive on ideals alone: you might also have financial targets of your own to hit.

Now you have two options. Option 1 is to help your audience get to their Profit goals and keep People and the Planet as the conduit for those. Here, you'll need to keep your own end of the bargain clear (including your non-negotiables from each of the three aspects, where applicable). Or, for Option 2, you can influence them to embed sustainability in their current and future business strategy so that it becomes another key performance indicator, alongside Profit.

Having reflected on these issues for a long time, I have reached the conclusion that, for me, it doesn't matter if people want more money, to look good in front of their customers or to blow their own trumpet on their marketing materials, while I want a more equitable society and a more liveable Planet.

The destination, the result, will be the same, but the reasons for reaching that destination will be different. Of course, in an ideal world, I would love to convert all the oil magnates into sustainability advocates. While the chances of that happening in the short term and as a result of one person's efforts are very slim, collective efforts and chipping away at it at every opportunity will eventually do that: oil magnates will feel cornered and will need to pivot towards sustainability. Historical data confirm that when at least 3.5% of the population mobilizes towards a certain issue, if conditions are right, chances are that the powers-to-be will take notice and act.[79] However, the situation is increasingly worrying and we need every single effort to get to that destination quickly even if, for some, the intentions are not as pure as we would like them to be.

The experience of most sustainability professionals I spoke to is that sustainability is either an afterthought or has been taken into consideration in one project only, as a sort of token to the proportion of customers that pay attention to these issues (for instance, one "environmentally friendly"[80] shampoo bar among hundreds of beauty products containing potentially toxic substances).

But there are several advantages for everyone involved in persuading your audience that the three Ps together are a crucial, strategic move: ensuring longevity for the business and accessing new funding, revenue streams and customer pools are only a few of the potential benefits.[81] If sustainability gets embedded in your audience's business and becomes their "business as usual", it will have the potential to unlock many untapped business opportunities that aren't available to them and competitors are already benefiting from.

This can also be the most advantageous solution for your own business, from a motivational point of view (you'll make a real difference) and

---

[79] Chenoweth, E. (2020). Questions, answers and some cautionary updates regarding the 3.5% rule. Carr Center Discussion Paper. Carr Center for Human Rights Harvard Kennedy School.

[80] Fun fact: when I lectured at university, I told my students that I'd take points off their grades if they used "environmentally friendly" in their papers. Nothing is vaguer and has a more greenwash feel than this expression.

[81] See Appendix C for more.

an economic one, as it might be a bigger deal than providing the bare minimum of support for a single project.

It can be argued that in today's VUCA[82] world, it pays to adopt sustainability as a key driving strategy. Several studies in recent years have looked at the increasing average global temperatures, paired with flooding and less rainfall, and their impact on crop yield: maize, wheat, sunflowers and summer fruit are all threatened by these events. Shortage of maize, for instance, has a knock-on effect on animal feeding and all the industries that currently depend on it, from food to leather. Shortage of timber because of warmer temperatures in Scandinavia where most of the European timber is grown has already been causing issues for the construction industry. The Western economy, increasingly relying on workforces in other parts of the world, which are often the most affected by extreme weather events, can be seriously disrupted. Insurance and banks have already taken notice and will not support businesses that do not look at their long-term strategies and do not have contingency plans in place. Even the gas and oil industry, which is currently breaking its promise to investors to defossilize and increase investments in renewable energy sources, will soon have to shift.[83]

Any business can be affected by the changing climate before it is possible to adapt.

I believe we are on the verge of real change. On the outside, it is frustrating to witness the lack of commitment from governments and industry, paired up with increasingly visible climate change signs, but your job when you communicate sustainability is also to convey this message:

<hr>

[82] The term VUCA, coined by Warren Bennis and Burt Nanus in 1985 and later adopted by the US Army War College, stands for Volatility, Uncertainty, Complexity, and Ambiguity. It describes the challenging conditions faced in leadership and management. Each element of VUCA represents different challenges: rapid change, unpredictability, interconnected factors, and unclear information. Understanding VUCA helps leaders adapt to a constantly evolving environment, emphasizing the need for flexibility and values-based decision-making. www.vuca-world.org/where-does-the-term-vuca-come-from/
[83] US news from *The Guardian* (2023, July 16). www.theguardian.com/us-news/2023/jul/16/big-oil-climate-pledges-extreme-heat-fossil-fuel

It is more and more a necessity, not a luxury, to shift to sustainable and regenerative business models.

The goals then can shift from "Let's use a green shade on our ads so that customers think we are sustainable" to "Let's look at what we believe in, the way we do business, who we hire to sit in our board so that it all aligns to a business model that can ensure the business' and the Planet's longevity".

But how can we persuade our audience of that?

Hone the art of persuasion

Greek philosopher Aristotle's teachings around the art of persuasion are still a great starting point for anyone willing to try them, even more than 2,400 years after they were formulated.

Aristotle talks about three fundamental elements that need to be present in a persuasive speech: *ethos* (integrity), *logos* (logic) and *pathos* (emotions). Let's see how these can apply to your sustainability conversations.

Ethos

This is about demonstrating your credibility and trustworthiness, hopefully already clear from Step 1.

- Social proof is important here. Share testimonials or the results that you have obtained by helping others in a similar situation as your current audience.

- Be clear about the steps to take and the timescales, pre-empting possible objections, showing that you have already done the work to understand their business well.

- Listen without interrupting. Nothing will build up trust more than active listening.

- Make those you are communicating with the hero of the conversation. Pay attention to them and find genuine reasons for smiling at them and making sure they feel like key contributors to the conversation. Avoid delivering a monologue.

Logos

This will appeal especially to the *Compliant/Dominant* personalities, but it will also be helpful to include in any proposal to justify an investment with their board.

- Provide proof that sustainability is safe and twice as advantageous as your audience's current business model,[84] in response to doubts about *Certainty*.

- Provide a full spread of advantages of adopting sustainability, from return on investment, to risk management to growth opportunities. Ensure these are not generic but tailored to their specific needs.[85]

- Showcase other companies that have embraced sustainability at a strategic level and succeeded in making it a reality – use examples that are relevant to your audience, considering factors like maturity of the company, location and type of business.

Pathos

Arousing emotions, especially positive ones, will make you memorable because these emotions will release oxytocin in your audience's brains, strengthening the bond and encouraging a positive disposition towards you.

- Rethink your case studies. You can make them a lot more interesting and elicit emotions (whether that's interest, sympathy or amusement) if you share the challenges you have gone through to get to the final result and any lessons learned. Showing your case studies as if everything was plain sailing is not only unrealistic (and it will raise suspicions that you are not telling the truth) but also boring. In every good Hollywood movie, there is at least one plot

---

[84] It has been demonstrated that, in order to switch to a new product or way of working, the new solution needs to be on average twice as good as the old one. Novemsky, N., and Kahneman, D. (2005). The boundaries of loss aversion. *Journal of Marketing Research*, 42(2), 119–128.

[85] Appendix C contains a list of value-creating advantages of adopting sustainability that you can use as a starting point to build up your business case.

twist the audience wasn't expecting at all – a challenge, which the hero of the story overcomes.

In your case study, did funds run out mid-way through the project? Did top management change their mind? Was an external circumstance the reason why production stopped – COVID for instance?

A twist in the plot generates interest even in business presentations or research papers. It also communicates the genuine struggles that make us humans, lowering the audience's barriers as they resonate with them.

But the important element here is to share *what you did* to support your previous clients to overcome their challenges. What actions did you take? What results did you get? How did your clients make more money, enhance their reputation, and win awards as a result? Remember, you are the sage supporting the hero, your audience, like Merlin to Arthur (aka Wart) in the *Sword in the Stone* Disney classic. And sustainability is the magic you use to make it happen.

- Emotions only come up when what you are sharing is relevant to your audience. That could be something you have in common with them or a professional experience that is parallel to theirs.

- If you are presenting a slide deck, consider opening it with a funny, curious, awe-inducing or relatable story. Something to pique their interest from the start, as opposed to the classic "This is who I am; this is what my company does". In a recent event I attended on systems change in the built environment, the host started their presentation with a picture of lichens and explained how these are an amazing example of a symbiotic relationship between algae and fungi the built environment could learn from to create truly sustainable human habitats.[86] Nine months on, I still remember that presentation because of its unconventional opening.

---

[86] If you are curious to know how lichen is similar to the built environment, the gist of their presentation was that just like lichen, construction projects are part of a larger ecosystem, and their interconnectedness is crucial. Effective change requires all parts to evolve together, recognizing and embracing mutual dependencies. Projects should emulate lichen by being regenerative and adaptive, efficiently utilizing resources and accommodating diverse conditions.

I think it is pretty obvious here that none of this can be done without adequate preparation. But we know how life can catch us unprepared. So my suggestion is to prepare a few stories, examples, case studies and logical arguments that you can quickly adapt according to the audience's personality and situation in advance. If you always work with the same kind of clients, this should be relatively easy to do.

Let's now see what else you can do to have the maximum chance of success to persuade people to go for more. Consider that you might need to try different strategies depending on the situation. The following strategies are all based on the SCARF (*Status, Certainty, Autonomy, Relatedness* and *Fairness*) model of social behaviour. When introducing a new concept, technology or idea, it is important to ensure that our audience feels they have got a fair deal that doesn't threaten their current *Status*, that won't impair their reputation, in which they have some decision power, with a clear pathway to get to positive results that are advantageous and personally relevant to them.

Get top management's commitment

One fundamental step that you will always need to take is to *involve the very top of the company in the key decisions* – especially if you want them to embed sustainability at a strategic level.

As we have seen from Step 1 (at the beginning of Part 3) and the work you have done to identify relevant stakeholders, top management may not actually be the key *promoters* of sustainability (those with power and interest in it). This is where stakeholder mapping comes very useful: *Which other stakeholders can you involve that can help you champion sustainability with top management?*

In those cases in which top management are *promoters* you'll need to get them on board as early in the process as possible so that you can ensure sustainability is integrated rather than being a bolt-on afterthought.

If top management is not who you are dealing with you need to ensure they are completely on board nevertheless, they are fully involved and committed to change.[87] This might mean presenting directly to them,

---

[87] In Step 5 we will look at how to elicit commitment from top management.

asking them for their opinions (which ensures their *Status* is taken into consideration) and working through the initial rejections by identifying the barriers and chipping at them one by one – as I'll explain in Step 4 of this framework. This work takes grit, but so long as the goals are clear and genuinely what's best for your audience, you'll get there.

Start small

I know you want your audience to embrace sustainability at a strategic level, but the shift from nothing to a complete rehaul of their core business might be too big. Can they explore sustainability in one aspect of their business, with the intention to roll it out to the rest of their business if the experiment is successful?

Offering free trial periods, charging less for a new product, launching one pilot product to see how well it sells… In consumer goods businesses, this is a very common way to enthuse people to get used to a new product/system and lower the barrier of resistance before committing to a fully fledged solution.

All of these can be very successful strategies that provide some form of *Certainty* around an unproven new system that is going to revolutionize business as usual. It's also "a foot in the door" that will make fully embracing sustainability easier in the future.

Offer a limited choice of options

Offering fewer choices of potential solutions you'll be happy with anyway helps with lowering your audience's resistance to letting go of the good old ways of doing business *(Certainty)*, and at the same time, it provides them with a sense of *Autonomy* because they are taking the decisions, not you (they are the heroes!). That also maintains their *Status* intact.

Be ready to explain why some options are better than others for them, even though on the surface they may look similar. This sort of detail will be appreciated especially by those with *Compliant* and *Steady* character traits.

Finally, make sure you include a "do nothing" option, and show the consequences of it. This will raise awareness in your audience on how the status quo might be, in fact, not a responsible long-term choice.

Be transparent and manage expectations

To increase *Certainty* (and your credibility too), be clear and transparent about the process and its risks: what it entails, the steps needed to reach that goal and the intermediate milestones, how much it will cost and what support you can offer.

Then ensure they take ownership of the process by inviting them to think about who will be responsible for what, potential risks, planned reviews and what systems they'll put in place to demonstrate continuous improvement.

No man is an island

Your audience might ask some legitimate questions about how sustainability is being implemented in the market, and about potential implications for their existing customers and staff. This is about *Relatedness* with others. Be prepared to do your research beforehand about all the potential stakeholders' reactions and implications. Ask yourself:

What are their competitors doing?

How would existing customers take the new direction the company might embrace?

How would the employees react?

Think about the advantages of such a move: would the company's new sustainable outlook attract better talent? A wider customer base made of newer generations? Are their competitors already taking steps to become more sustainable (in which case this would be an excellent incentive for change and a compelling case study)? Can this company lead the way and attract the attention of the media?

Be ready to manage change

Virtually no one likes change. That's how our species has preserved and evolved so well in the last four million years. Sure, we have peaks of innovation here and there, but if you think about everyday life, it's Groundhog Day repeating itself most of the time. So, when change *must happen*, we struggle with it. We think it's not *Fair*. In reality, we as a species are remarkably good at adapting. It's just that we sometimes don't see it because it takes time to accept change and adapt from disruption to a new order.

In most aspects of life, disruption is followed by disorder and chaos until, slowly but surely, a new emerging order takes place, and it becomes the new system. People naturally go through all the emotions, from shock and disbelief to denial to anger to acceptance and, finally, to seeing opportunity and embracing the new order.[88]

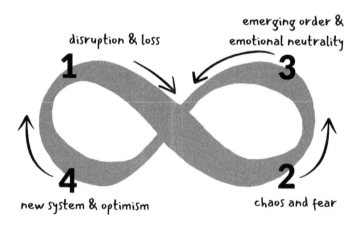

Figure 11 Change and its emotional components

In the heat of the moment, most people don't see how things can be different from the status quo they are used to, so the question for you here is: *How can you make it fairer for them?*

---

[88] Leadership consultant Jim McNeish developed this model, which is represented as an infinite symbol to depict the continuous nature of change and the emotional flow through all the states. https://neish.co/change/

You'll need to offer your support in handling the moments of transition sensitively and by focusing on people. You can acknowledge the achievements of the company until this point, and the positive legacy of the previous system. You can identify opportunities in the new system and share with them the big picture. You can help them create temporary structures during the transition – perhaps with templates, extra information and examples on how to transition to the new system quicker. You can encourage dialogue and collaboration.

SMART goals for success

In Step 2, you have worked with your audience to set goals they'll want to pursue, whether ambitious and strategic, or specific to a project or even a single conversation in line with their needs. Now you'll need to ensure the goals are SMART (*Specific, Measurable, Attainable, Realistic* and *Timebound*) and that there is a plan in place to make them happen.

I've seen plenty of sustainability teams (and even countries!) setting Net Zero goals for 2050 without scoping out a roadmap to get there with measurable steps and milestones, intermediate checkpoints, systems to experiment and get feedback, or even assigning responsibilities.

A goal without a plan is just a wish.

Antoine de Saint-Exupéry

"Net Zero by 2050" is not a goal that inspires or gets people excited to help make it a reality – and this can be a factor contributing to the lack of specific plans. I'm not saying it's not a worthwhile goal, but that it can be expressed differently to have a higher chance of being endorsed by all stakeholders and to be achieved.

First of all, what does Net Zero mean? Lots of people don't know. Can we express it differently? Do we want the company to reduce its carbon impact as much as possible and find meaningful ways to offset whatever carbon emissions it still produces? Also, is 2050 the right deadline or is it what everyone else is aiming at? Can we be ambitious and set the goals for the end of the next decade? What does that look like in practice?

Step 3: Co-creation

*I*n *Step 2 you have set some meaningful goals with your audience to address their issues. Now it's time to co-create the solutions.*

Co-creation means making that delicious cake I mentioned at the beginning of the book by contributing a few ingredients each.

We need to take for granted that we are all intelligent and resourceful beings and that we trust we can address the issues at hand together. When we are determined to co-create sustainability with someone else to reach common and individual goals, we need to assess what we can each contribute to the discussion. For instance, you provide your technical expertise, and they can give you invaluable insights into their business.

I come from the construction industry, and while in the UK it is an industry that has progressed significantly towards a more sustainable built environment in the last 30 years, it is also an industry that is carbon- and waste-intensive, and profoundly rooted in traditional practices. Smaller businesses in the field still struggle to adapt their construction processes to be more sustainable.

One of the issues that prevents sustainability from being adopted across the sector is the traditional way of working in silos. Architects do not usually talk with engineers until the design is pretty much finalized. Landscape architects, acousticians, life cycle assessors and other experts, manufacturers and subcontractors do not get involved until late in the project. Even now that technology is available in the form of shared cloud platforms and software to collaborate, only some projects are developed collaboratively.

Sustainability for many is the stereotypical photovoltaic panel stuck on the roof, while we know well that it's rather a way of thinking that needs to be embedded in the project even before the idea of a building is conceived: questions about location and whether to build new or refurbish determine how sustainable the final building will be.

When all the experts and relevant stakeholders have a chance to meet early on in a project and contribute their expertise to it, the result is cheaper, more innovative, sustainable and there are fewer issues down the line. A process such as this implies having a strong framework that ensures everyone's views are captured, discussed and taken into consideration, and different approaches are tested through a reiterative feedback loop system early in the project.

A co-created result will always be stronger as it will have a wider perspective and address any potential issues when it is more economical and easier to do so. How does that translate in other cases, and even in a single sustainability conversation?

The principles of co-creation

Last year I attended a webinar on Regenerative Architecture. During the Q&A I commented that, in order to obtain a regenerative built environment, we need to stop working in silos and aim at collaborating. The host, Martin Brown, an experienced regeneration expert, corrected me, saying:

> When working on sustainable and regenerative projects, we shouldn't aim at collaboration but at co-creation.

I have reflected a lot on this comment ever since and, in fact, these reflections have fundamentally changed the direction of this book.

Collaboration means working together, but each person is contributing their bit as asked. *Co-creation* implies a much greater sense of agency by everyone involved in the project, including the silent stakeholder, the Planet.

It implies that there isn't an expert dispensing their knowledge, but a collective intelligence coming together to create something better than the single contributions.

Let's see what process can be implemented to obtain a co-created outcome.

Principle 1: Openly invite others to co-create the outcomes and rules of the communication

In Step 1, you have mapped all the potential stakeholders that need to be involved in this conversation. Once every key stakeholder is around the table, explain that you are not trying to impose your views, but rather welcome a process in which everyone has a chance to share their ideas for a truly sustainable outcome, and that you'll do your best to facilitate that process and offer your expertise when needed. But a process like this, especially if it involves a large number of people, needs some ground rules.

How are you going to co-create?

People are more used to collaboration than co-creation. So make sure everyone understands the difference between the two and the advantages of co-creating (i.e., more fitting, innovative results and sense of ownership from everyone involved).

What systems/processes do you need to do that?

If it's a one-off sustainability conversation, this can be as simple as just inviting people to share their views in the discussion, and making sure that everyone has a chance to do so. Even adults sometimes need to be reminded to take turns.

In all the coaching courses I attended, at the start of the course the trainer would invite the participants to come up with some rules to add to a "contract" we all needed to abide by. The aim was to work together in the best possible way during the course. Each of us would share the rules we thought were important, like listening without interrupting, being empathetic, not judging, even having fun and so on. This made us feel like we all had agency over the course, that we weren't passive recipients of the trainer's knowledge, as we were shaping the course together. This can be done briefly in a conversation in which you have already agreed on some goals to achieve by the end of the conversation. It can be as simple as:

> *I think we will have a much better chance to achieve our goals if we take turns to share our ideas while I note them down, then we can share the pros and cons of each in turns, what do you think? Any other ideas on how we can work together in the best possible way?*

When you are setting up the discussion for a longer project, ground rules could be around when and how to collaborate.

> *Should we have a weekly 30-minute round-robin meeting, and then use a messaging platform to discuss daily issues?*

> *Would everyone prefer a daily catch-up or communicating via an online task management system?*

> *Where will the information and outcomes from each interaction be stored?*

If several people must be involved as identified in the stakeholder mapping exercise (for instance, the customers of a bank could be asked about their opinion on the most important issues under the ESG umbrella), should you:

> *Do sample interviews?*

> *Send a survey?*

> *Invite a few to a workshop?*

Before I worked with them, a client of mine had three different channels of communication for their six-person team and their clients: WhatsApp, emails and Microsoft Teams, with no specific rules about which channels to use for what and when. Clients would send emails to their account manager's inbox; as a consequence, others who worked on the same project had no way of accessing information especially if the account manager was away for any reason. Additionally, information didn't get systematically stored in a central depository and wasn't accessible to everyone. Sometimes the team would exchange Teams messages about the project, which would just be forgotten, and information was lost in a flurry of messages about other issues. You can see that a system like this is *not* efficient and can cause considerable damage, including loss of important information, delays and errors.

On the other hand, another consultancy company I worked with a few years ago had separate email addresses for each of the many projects they were consulting on, the IDs of which were the unique project names used in their database's folders. Any client communication happened via email using those specific project email addresses to leave a trail of evidence. On receiving it, all important information sent by clients via email was immediately transferred to the database in the project folders. The database and email inboxes were accessible by all the staff, so if the account manager of a specific project wasn't around, anyone else would be able to find any information if needed. Both internal communication and client meetings happened via Teams, so that they could be recorded and the transcripts saved in the database too. Finally, they had templates for everything from meeting minutes to project trackers, so that there was consistency across projects and information was easy to retrieve.

If we want open communication and collaboration, it's important to enable it in a way that doesn't create friction, allows everyone to have an equal voice and important information is handled carefully in the process.

Use *Yes... and* to generate innovative ideas together

Yes... and is a classic improvisation comedy technique that allows actors to co-create scenarios by building on each other's ideas with often hilarious results as they become more and more absurd. Accepting every idea as at least partially valid, even when wacky, means that everyone feels validated and included and as a consequence, less intimidated to share more ideas. Dismissing other actors' ideas, on the other hand, would halt the creative process and create an impasse in the comedy scene.

The *Yes... and* principles can be applied successfully to our sustainability conversations to innovate our collective thinking. Sometimes ideas just need to flow to become innovative, even if the first few are absurd or unviable. Presenting objections at the start stops this creative co-creation process.

This doesn't mean that you have to say "yes" to everything. But I invite you to switch from a default *No* to the potential hidden in *Yes... and*. In particular, I invite you to assume that the other person is *at least 10% right* and focus on that 10% as opposed to what's wrong with their ideas.

Author Bob Kulhan[89] suggests that leaders often think too analytically, focusing on problems instead of seeing opportunities. The *Yes... and* approach – accepting ideas (at least partially) and building on them - encourages creativity and adaptability. This fosters a positive, fearless environment where ideas can flourish because of the shared understanding that it is okay for ideas to fail, and it is okay for people to take chances.

You practically implement the *Yes... and* technique by listening attentively, and being flexible and open to possibilities. So you could say:

> *What I like about that idea is...* [mention the 10% that you think is right] *AND...* [add another idea that's triggered by what you liked]

For example, imagine you are in a marketing meeting with a colleague:

> **Colleague:** How about starting a plastic-free campaign with a festival for the community, with Carnival-like carriages representing the monsters of pollution?

> **You:** *What I like about your idea is* the community aspect of a plastic-free campaign. It will give us great visibility and we can really use it as an opportunity to educate the local kids. *And* we could involve the schools as well.

> **Colleague:** *Yes! And* we could focus on sustainable alternatives to packaged snacks and offer awareness sessions to the children.

> **You:** Great idea! We could even get sponsorship from the local bakery.

Notice how you have glossed over the Carnival idea and focused on the element you thought was more viable. From the flamboyant idea of putting together an expensive Carnival event, using *Yes... and* has

---

[89] Kulhan, B. (2017). *Getting to "Yes And": The Art of Business Improv.*

quickly generated better ideas and great opportunities for partnerships, visibility and support to local schools.[90]

You can continue with the *Yes... and* technique until you gather a large quantity of ideas (*divergent thinking*). Only then move on to evaluating and editing the ideas that are actually worth pursuing (*convergent thinking*) for effective innovation.

Why not add this technique to the ground rules of meetings and workshops?

At this point you might ask: *But how can you implement this idea when you are in a conversation with someone who doesn't know about Yes... and?*

Imagine the MD of a small company has agreed to meet you but they are obviously not so keen to implement sustainability in their company at the moment.

Potential client: I think looking at sustainability would be a good idea, but right now we don't have the resources. (*They are putting up the first barrier: resources.*)

You: I'm pleased to hear that you are open to the idea of introducing sustainability in your company. *And* I'm sure I can help you explore the options available to you, even with limited resources. (*You don't dismiss their concerns, but focus on the small opening they provided you and build on that by offering support to overcome the specific barrier they put up.*)

Potential client: Oh, I never thought that would be possible on a low budget... but I don't think we have time before the next financial year to introduce anything new. (*Second barrier: time.*)

You: *Yes*, time is quite tight, *and* I can show you how we have been working with other clients in a similar situation and implemented sustainability gradually. Our team helped them every step of the way with templates and one-to-one support. We only need a couple of hours of your time to start with. (*Again, you don't*

---

[90] There would be nothing wrong with saying out loud: "*I'm not sure about the Carnival carriages*" after you have endorsed part of your colleague's idea, as they should already feel validated.

dismiss their concerns, but build on those by offering an alternative to the cumbersome and expensive process this prospective client imagines.)

Potential client: Great, if you can make it work for me with the constraints I have, we can definitely keep the conversation going. In particular, I'd love to look at our operations' impact…

You can see from this scenario how not embracing the negative response from the person in front of you, while it hasn't generated lots of new ideas, has shifted the conversation towards a positive outcome. Again, listening attentively to what is being said and building up on the positive nuggets that might emerge can transform the conversation and open up unexpected possibilities.

(Another) few words about meetings

By now you'll know my opinion about the misuse of meetings. But here I want to add one more important aspect to watch out for. More often than not, meetings do not offer the most conducive environment to our best thinking.

If you want your sustainability conversations to really get the best out of people, consider *how* you can improve the way meetings take place.

Fact: brains need novelty to get creative.[91]

Here are a few ideas to take advantage of this.

- Encourage people to move either before the meeting or *during* the meeting. Especially if you have only a handful of attendees, an outdoor meeting while walking encourages creativity, especially if in a natural environment. Walking outside and detaching ourselves from our usual workplace for a while to slow down and have a break from technology and commitments, lower stress and make us think deeply and creatively: Nature can provide an infinite source of inspiration and stimuli.

---

[91] Gillebaart, M., Förster, J., Rotteveel, M., and Jehle, A. C. M. (2013). Unravelling effects of novelty on creativity. *Creativity Research Journal*, 25(3), 280–285; Medina, J. (2008). *Brain Rules: 12 Principles for Surviving and Thriving at Work, Home and School.*

Lots of great thinkers from Einstein to Darwin to Virginia Woolf, used to go on long walks before sitting down to work. Being outdoors and walking allows the brain to rest and recharge and encourages blood flow which helps bring oxygen to it.[92] Walking can shift the brainwaves from a fast-paced beta state, associated with higher anxiety and activity to a slower alpha-state, which fosters clearer thinking, problem-solving, and creativity.[93] Some research conducted at Stanford University in the USA demonstrated that creativity improves on average 60% after a walk.[94] But if you don't have access to the great outdoors, even having indoor plants or staring briefly at pictures of green environments can boost attention and concentration.[95]

- Find a different place to have your meeting. An art gallery or a quiet and quirky café can work well.

- Especially if your meeting is online, offer a re-energizing break every 50 minutes. Encourage people to take a comfort or coffee break, or step outside. Do a quick energizer. Tell a story. Share a quote or cartoon.

- Get people to co-create on a shared (virtual or physical) whiteboard. The act of engaging actively with a shared resource will encourage participation and innovative thinking.

Create a thinking environment. Often meetings are dominated by a few, extroverted characters. This can be enough to stop other, more introverted people from sharing their ideas.

---

[92] Experimental Biology (2017, April 24). How walking benefits the brain. ScienceDaily. www.sciencedaily.com/releases/2017/04/170424141340.htm

[93] Roberts, L. (2022). *Coaching Outdoors. The Essential Guide to Partnering with Nature in Your Coaching Conversations.*

[94] Oppezzo, M., and Schwartz, D. L. (2014). Give your ideas some legs: The positive effect of walking on creative thinking. *Journal of Experimental Psychology: Learning, Memory, and Cognition,* 40(4), 1142–1152.

[95] Lee, K. E. et al. (2015). 40-second green roof views sustain attention: The role of micro-breaks in attention restoration. *Journal of Environmental Psychology,* vol. 42, 182–189.

In order to encourage collective intelligence, you need to enable a *thinking environment*:[96] a safe space in which everyone takes turns sharing their ideas, knowing that they will not be interrupted. This will allow everyone to think faster and deeper. Listening actively is paramount here, and should be the first ground rule of any meeting.

A commitment to listening without interrupting and giving full attention to the speaker is the best way to enable people to share their best thoughts freely. You can also set up *thinking partnerships* of two people in which they can share for five minutes with each other without interrupting.

Allow questions only when everyone has taken their turns. Open questions are best. Some especially insightful questions, borrowed from the world of coaching, can stimulate deeper thinking:

What might we be assuming here that could be limiting our thinking?

If there were no obstacles, what would you do?

If it were entirely up to you, what would you like the situation to be?

And my favourite:

Is there anything more you think, feel or want to say?

This understated question often brings up real insights, so don't skip it!

Principle 2: Allow everyone to think outside the box

As I have explained earlier, inviting people to take a *systems thinking*[97] approach can unlock fresh ideas. Let me introduce you to a relatively simple way to think solutions through with your audience, which can stimulate a substantial pool of fit-for-purpose ideas: *causal loop diagrams*.[98]

---

[96] Kline, N. (1999). *Time to Think: Listening to Ignite the Human Mind.*

[97] In the spirit of the Good Communicator and striving for jargon-free communication, you might want to think twice before using the term *Systems Thinking*, as this can put people off very quickly. Opt for something like "big picture thinking" or "collaborative problem-solving".

[98] There are many resources online to better understand causal loop diagrams. These are some of the resources I found helpful: Gurule, D. (2018, January 4). *Systems Thinking: causal loop diagrams* [Video]. YouTube. www.youtube.com/watch?v=LgnBSdcxPD0 and

This is a systems thinking tool used in research as well as business strategy planning to identify the variables within a system and indicate the cause-effect relationships between them. By linking the loops that come out of such an exercise, a rich story will emerge about the issue, which will generate more apt solutions.

Let's build, in stages, a causal loop diagram based on a complex environmental issue that has been heavily featured in the UK media in recent years: the discharge of untreated sewage in watercourses by water utility companies.[99]

First: Identify the system

A system is defined by the Merriam-Webster dictionary as "a regularly interacting or interdependent group of items forming a unified whole". To identify this system, I'm going to ringfence the issue as expressed by an article published on the BBC News website in January 2024: "The number of hours in which sewage was dumped into the River Thames has more than quadrupled in the last year."[100]

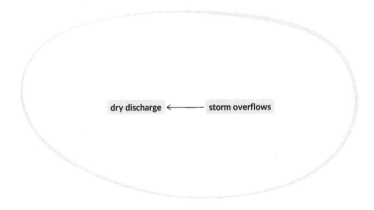

Figure 12 *The events that shape this system*

Lannon, C. (2016, January 14). *Causal Loop Construction: The Basics – the Systems Thinker.* https://thesystemsthinker.com/causal-loop-construction-the-basics/
[99] To build this causal loop diagram, I'm using public information from a reputable news outlet, BBC News.
[100] BBC News (2024, January 24). *Thames Water sewage spills more than quadruple, data shows.* www.bbc.co.uk/news/articles/cx0vk2d4wvgo

We could make this as wide as we like and include many other factors, but for the sake of this exercise, I'm limiting the system to this issue and all the *variables* around it, including its connected *causes* and *consequences*.

A bit of background: the Thames Valley, in which London sits, is the most populated area of the UK. Thames Water is the water utility company which at the time of writing serves approximately 16 million people living in the area by both providing fresh water and dealing with wastewater.

Discharging untreated wastewater in rivers and sea coastlines is allowed by UK environmental legislation but only as an emergency measure when there is an overflow of water in the system due to heavy rain. Although not ideal, in such cases, the excess rainwater dilutes the raw sewage and the impact is lessened. However, the company has been under scrutiny because it has been discharging raw sewage in high volumes in dry weather periods. In some instances, this water company discharged over 2 billion litres of raw sewage in the River Thames in the space of two days.

Second: Identify the variables

In the causal loop diagram (see Figure 13), I drew the possible *causes* of this event.

These are my *variables*, i.e. elements that change over time, and that either go in the same direction as the issue or in the opposite direction. To identify them, I ask questions such as:

> *What's the cause of this issue?*
>
> *How does this cause influence the issue?*
>
> *If the cause grows over time, does it grow (goes in the same direction) or reduce (goes in the opposite direction)?*

For instance, the more the population grows in the Thames Valley, the more the system is put under pressure by the increased volume of sewage and the more storm overflow episodes occur. So, the possible cause/variable "population growth" goes in the same direction as the event "storm overflows".

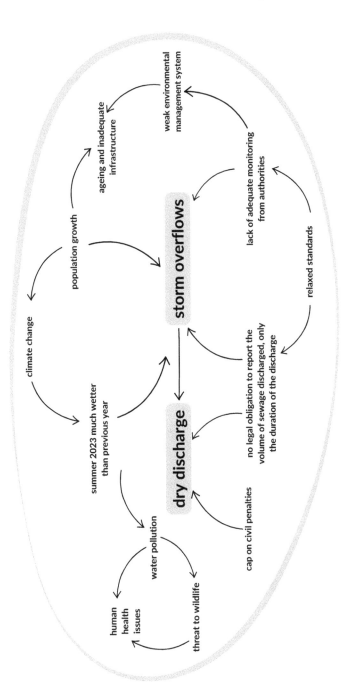

Figure 13 The potential causes (variables) of the events and their interconnections

As we draw the diagram, additional factors emerge that influence the issue at hand: e.g. Summer 2023 was wetter than the previous summer; the water infrastructure is ageing and inadequate. However, under closer scrutiny and after reading several articles on this fact, other possible and compounding causes emerge, connected to the legislative and public administration scenario: the UK standards on storm overflows are not strict enough; there is a cap on civil penalties for such incidents; monitoring of breaches is patchy; the companies are under no obligation to disclose the volume of sewage discharged, just the duration of the discharge. This means that, for water companies, it is more convenient to pay the penalties and continue to discharge raw sewage in the watercourses (which, by the way, is almost certainly more than estimated given the lack of efficient measuring systems) than invest in infrastructure improvements.

The consequences of this issue, also variables in this system, are severe for both human health and wildlife.[101]

Third: Connect the variables

This is where system thinking kicks in. The more you look at the variables, the more you see causal connections. This is where some "loops" start to emerge. When you close a loop between connections, you can label it (in this example we have a legislative/policing loop, an environmental management loop, a climate change loop, and a pollution vs. health loop). This is where we start making sense of the wider system connections, and where some macro-issues emerge. (See Figure 14.)

Fourth: Think about changes and trends over time

How have these variables and their connections changed over time?

What will happen if one or more of those changes in the future?

---

[101] I have chosen not to include in the diagram a few more connections and facts (including that Thames Water has initially refused to share data about the discharge) for the sake of brevity, but hopefully the ones I did include provide a good enough picture of the value of this exercise.

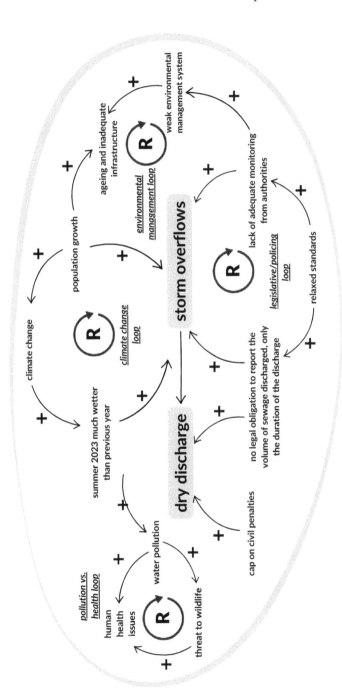

Figure 14 Reinforcing loops (underlined) emerge by connecting the variables

These two questions reveal reinforcing or balancing *trends*: either the issue increases or decreases over time ("R" on the diagram), or stays the same ("B", which we have none of here). In our scenario, population has grown over time, and this meant increasingly more unpredictable and heavier weather events – this connection has a "+" next to it indicating that one element reinforces the other – with more frequent and heavier storm overflow incidents. Overall, this indicates a growing trend.

Hypothetically, if monitoring of the infrastructure increases in frequency and effectiveness perhaps via investment in digital monitoring systems and more audits, the water company's environmental management system will become more robust, which will force them to look after and modernize the existing infrastructure. In turn, storm overflow incidents will reduce with positive knock-on effects on the other elements of the system, assuming all the other elements stay the same. In this case, the current negative trend would stop.

Fifth: Talk through the loop

Once you are satisfied all the connections have been drawn, tell the story that emerges, making sure that you highlight the trends, behaviours and even mindsets behind this system. This will draw attention to any fallacies but also clarify the system to everyone involved.

In this case, the lack of legislative control and penalties has allowed those in charge to game the system and avoid taking the environmental damage seriously – I'm stopping here as I know I could go down a rabbit hole of deprecation of the current Profit-over-Planet-and-People mindset prevailing in the business world...

Sixth: Co-create the solutions

Thames Water has responded to criticisms by declaring that the new Thames Tideway Tunnel, a 25km "super-sewer" under the river, will intercept spills and help clean up the river.

Do you think, having analysed the complexity of this system and interconnected issues, that such a solution will be sufficient to address the *root causes* of the problem?

What about improving monitoring of the infrastructure; a more efficient environmental management system; transparent Governance; commitment to continuous improvements to the existing infrastructure; lobbying to change the legislation towards stricter standards and controls; and rethinking the current system of dealing with overloading of the infrastructure in the scenario of increasing changing climate events?

As you can see, a causal loop diagram can highlight several areas in which multiple solutions are needed to address the causes, not just the *symptoms* of the issues.

Having all the co-creators around a whiteboard thinking together by using this tool enables their brains to synchronize and generate more insights and ideas than simply listing what we know about the issue and what caused it.

To get familiar with this tool, why not choose a headline from the news a day – or a week – and sketch a causal loop diagram while having your morning coffee? This will increase your capacity to see the multiple consequences of our actions and the interconnectedness of our world through new eyes.

From insight to action: leveraging causal diagrams to enhance the ESG strategy

Amit A, who we met earlier in the book, is the Head of ESG and Sustainability at a medium design and construction company.

Last year I managed to persuade our managing directors that the market for sustainable construction was expanding and that we needed to have a sustainability team (as opposed to just me as sustainability manager) to grab this opportunity and meet the growing demands from our clients.

I got promoted as Head of ESG and Sustainability but I soon realized that our newly formed small team of three was already struggling to meet the expectations and the ambitious targets we had set for ourselves at the beginning of this new adventure: we wanted to provide sustainability training to our colleagues, deliver certification services to our clients, and had other ambitious projects around classification of materials and making our building sites as sustainable as possible.

Facilitated by Green Gorilla, we reassessed our situation together as a team using a causal loop diagram. We found a number of causes of our struggles: from increasing demands for our services, both from our colleagues in other departments and external clients, to limited budgets, to unclear responsibilities and priorities.

Drawing the diagram together helped us identify the two root causes: lack of planning; and lack of top management commitment. These were also reinforcing trends that were causing chaos and stress in the team.

We realized that our managing directors had profit as their main goal and had yet to make the connection between sustainability and the business opportunities it can provide – we had to change their mindset in order to make our team function as intended.

Ultimately, this was my job as the Head of ESG and Sustainability to deal with. I had to focus on providing the full picture of sustainability to the managing directors so that they could see not just the ethical side of it, but also the business case for it. If they did, they would invest more resources into our team; crucially, we needed them to budget for more staff.

I also realized I had to rein in the enthusiasm of the team (and mine!) and prioritize the most important, money-earning activities in the short-term, as they would be added proof for our top management team that we were not an overhead but a profitable business unit.

Facilitated by Green Gorilla, we held a full team strategy day to plan for the year ahead, where we took some tough decisions to temporarily park some interesting projects, and defined the steps for those projects we had to deliver as a priority in line with our mission, values and goals.

Principle 3: Plan on how to tackle the solutions

Let's go back to our supermarket chain example at the beginning of this part of the book.

You have worked with the supermarket's directors to review their EV fleet initial ideas, and, to reach zero-carbon in their delivery operations, have devised an affordable ten-year plan to improve operational efficiency of their deliveries by 50% and change all their vehicles to electric (and/or any new renewable fuel technology that might become available in the meantime) in stages. A systematic review of their operations and systems using the techniques shared so far will help identify areas of improvement and tackle both the low-hanging fruit (as a way to put a "foot in the door" as explained earlier) and the biggest issues that might require more complex planning and resources.

Working backwards from the goals established earlier, you'll see how your client will need to change the way they deliver their goods quite dramatically: to tackle their energy and carbon target they will need to look at the efficiency of the vehicles they currently use, the fuel used to power them, their delivery schedules and logistics plans, and their supply chain's emissions.

How to convey a complex scenario without overwhelm

The issue here is to manage the magnitude of the systemic changes your client needs to go through without scaring them away. The best way to do that is to break down such an overwhelming project into its basic structural components, explain clearly what they are, and offer to help throughout.

- Break the scope of the transformation they will have to go through into manageable steps. Involve them in this process by asking questions to understand their priorities and concerns about each step.

- How can you clarify the process for them? We have talked about the value of carefully selected case studies and examples. You should also make sure that responsibilities, deadlines and tasks for the following months are clear and assigned, that regular catch-ups are in the calendar, and that any shared information is stored in an accessible and secure place.

- You can offer to help in various ways, e.g. with technical support, templates, examples, training sessions, the big picture view, suggestions for restructuring the system for efficiency, further reading, or you can assign a project liaison within your team who will always be available to support your client and answer any questions.

Remember to be present. Listen actively and take any objections not as a personal attack, but as riddles to solve. Use your empathy to work out where the objections come from and respond accordingly.

How to prioritize solutions to reach the goals

Now that we know what we need to do, how do we close the gap between the current state and our desired outcome? This is where you can help by "backcasting" from the future vision goals instead of trying to fix today's issues. By fixing today's issues instead of focusing on realizing the long-term vision you will end up with a partial Frankenstein result, which will be outdated very quickly.

Priority should then be given to those actions that will take your audience closer to that ultimate goal fastest, as opposed to fixing short-term issues.

Let me introduce you, in stages, to a method to work out priorities: the multi-criteria prioritization table (see Figure 15).[102]

---

[102] My method is based on the Pugh Matrix, a decision-making tool originally developed for engineering design. Pugh, S. (1991). *Total Design: Integrated Methods for Successful Product Engineering*.

Issues	Actions	Potential solutions	Criteria Environmental and social impact	Budget	Relevance to stakeholders Customers	Staff	Reputation	Future adaptability	Final weighted scores
			30	20	20	20	5	5	100
- Carbon intensity of petrol/diesel vehicles - Air pollution - Maintenance and fuel costs - Competition has already upgraded	Continue	Use digital trackers to work out less carbon intensive routes and times	1	0	0	0	0	1	35
	Stop	Use petrol/diesel vans for daytime short and light deliveries	1	1	1	0	1	1	80
	Reduce	Use existing larger vans to night-time and bigger deliveries only	1	1	1	0	1	1	80
	Improve	Buy a few second-hand EVs for light/short distance deliveries	1	-1	1	0	1	1	40
		Retrofitted aerodynamic load spaces and trailers	1	-1	0	0	0	0	10
	Upskill	Training for drivers on fuel efficient driving	1	0	0	1	0	1	55
	Start	Think-tank with all major corporations to lower emissions of goods distribution from places of production to warehouses	1	0	0	0	1	1	40
		Involve the supermarket customers in lowering home-delivery emissions (e.g. website indicates lower emission options depending on time of day/location, like picking up vs. delivery)	1	0	0	0	1	1	40
	Innovate	Hydrogen vehicles and delivery drones (when available)	1	-1	0	0	0	1	15

Figure 15 Multi-criteria prioritization table

Potential impact legend (compared to status quo)
1 positive change (short term)
-1 negative change or significant costs involved
0 situation unchanged

First: Choose your criteria. Think through with your audience which specific criteria to use to compare the possible solutions to address their issues and reach their goals. Consider the three Ps as you do so, e.g.:

- environmental and social impact
- urgency
- budget
- return on investment (ROI)
- risks
- alignment with the company's mission
- relevance to the stakeholders
- reputation
- innovation
- future adaptability
- marketing opportunities.

Use your evaluation criteria as a starting point, but keep in mind that these might shift as time goes by. This exercise is purely a jumping-off point for analysis and decision-making rather than a final step.

In our fictional supermarket chain scenario, the criteria might be environmental and social impact, budget, relevance to stakeholders, reputation and future adaptability.

Second: Give each of the criteria a weighted score out of 100. This will help determine which criteria are more relevant at this point in time and in the specific context.[103]

Third: Line up the possible solutions. To generate ideas, ask the audience what they can *Continue, Stop, Reduce, Improve, Upskill on, Start* or *Innovate* to reduce the negative and increase the positive impacts on the three Ps.

For instance, is the size and efficiency of their vehicles commensurate to the number of deliveries and distance they have to cover? Could they *improve* their current fleet with a few electric vans for day-time

---

[103] The weighting is entirely up to you and the other stakeholders, and what you collectively think is relatively more important, depending on the specific business and circumstances. In the example, for argument's sake, I weighted Environmental and Social Impact 30%, Budget 20%, Reputation 5% and so on.

short distance deliveries, while *reducing* older diesel vehicles usage to less congested night deliveries only?

Fourth: Evaluate one by one the potential solutions against the criteria in your selection matrix. Ask whether each will bring a positive (1) or negative change (-1), or whether things will stay as they currently are (0). How you score is entirely up to you and other stakeholders involved: the scope of this process is to help discuss the issues in more depth. For example, smaller petrol vans may work better under the "environmental and social impact" column for small loads and short distance deliveries than current large lorries, so that would be marked as "1" on the chart; however, this wouldn't change significantly the situation for staff, so that's marked as "0" on the chart under the "relevance to stakeholders (staff)" column.

The impact of future innovative technologies like hydrogen vehicles and delivery drones is currently unknown, but we can hypothesize that in the timescale we are looking at (ten years) they will probably be expensive to start with (marked as "-1" in the "budget" column on the chart) and we can take an educated guess as to what impact they'd have on customers (marked as "0" as it probably won't matter to people how their groceries are delivered).

Fifth: Weigh your findings to determine the highest priority. Once you've marked up all the solutions against the criteria as positive, negative or neutral, multiply each score by the weight given to each criterion, then sum them up in the "Weighted rating" column.

Tentatively speaking, the solutions with the highest scores on the matrix are the highest priority and should be looked at first (in our example, using smaller vehicles for daytime and larger ones for night-time deliveries, followed by training drivers). The others can then be planned for the future.

However, one good way of building momentum with your audience is to think about immediate actions (in the following three months to a year). Sustainability changes rapidly, so flexibility and adaptability are an important part of the overall plan: a combination of short-term planned actions and regular check-in points throughout the journey will ensure the long-term goals are still relevant over time.

If you are dealing with a particularly forward-thinking audience, they might want to tackle the systemic changes head on. In our example, urban goods deliveries are predicted to rise by 78% through 2030. Do we still want thousands of fossil fuel-powered vans in the streets to get groceries in people's homes, or can we think of more innovative and wide-ranging ways to reduce the massive impact of this phenomenon, perhaps by joining forces with other players in the industry to rethink the whole foods delivery ecosystem?

Take this exercise as simply a way to stimulate the discussion around priorities, and the reasons why some solutions are worth investing in before, or instead of, others. To further define the initial steps to take, you can ask some additional questions:

What is the most important first step you can take in the next three months to move the project forward?

Who will be responsible for it?

When will you review this action to ensure you are on track and the goals are still meaningful?

What KPIs can you employ to demonstrate you are on track?

How is this particular action going to affect other stakeholders involved and the wider goals?

What are the potential risks and opportunities?

What systems and resources do you need to put in place to make it happen?

How is this action going to affect or be affected by the ethos and values of your business?

Hopefully through this process you can see how backcasting from the end goals is not about slapping on quick fixes to make the current reality marginally better. It's about getting creative and addressing the root causes head-on.

What to do when projects lack ambition

You might be asking at this point: *What if I haven't managed to get my audience to buy into a long-term vision yet?*

The same principles apply to projects that are a little less ambitious – in the quest for a better future, every little helps. You can take the same long-term approach even if the project is limited in scope.

The main question to ask your audience is: *If not now, when?*

For instance, if the supermarket chain didn't want to change their delivery operations in their entirety, can they start from the solutions that can provide the best "benefits vs. cost and effort" value, then commit to continuous improvement over time to reach their goals? For example:

- Can they improve the vehicles' maintenance programme so that they run as designed?

- Can they change the schedules to ensure deliveries are more fuel and time efficient?

- Can they train staff on fuel efficient driving?

In any case, it is worth asking:

> *How are you planning to progressively reduce carbon in the next ten years?*
>
> *What steps can you take, by when, to get there?*
>
> *What KPIs will you use to measure success?*

To ensure the goals are still relevant and the trajectory to reach them is still the most appropriate, such an exercise should be repeated on a regular basis as business priorities and other market influencing factors shift.

The importance of commitment and accountability

There are plenty of frameworks out there that can help structure the adoption of sustainability, not least an environmental management system like ISO14001 or one of the many ESG frameworks available on the market, but essentially, they all share the same sequence of steps: *Plan – Do – Check – Act*.

In my experience, unless there is some accountability, for instance by applying for or renewing a certification, a company will *Plan* and partially *Do*, then fail to *Check* and *Act/Adjust*. Conflicting priorities, changes in leadership, political and economic scenarios, and day-to-day firefighting can easily take over good intentions, especially if there isn't a firm commitment from the top management to make it a priority.

As sustainability leaders, we need to make sure there is commitment *and* systems around the goals as well as a Plan B, or else sustainability will fall by the wayside at the first hurdle.

We will look at ways to ensure commitments are followed through in the final step of the framework (Step 5).

Principle 4: Implement feedback loops

As we have seen, sustainability is not well communicated at the moment: learning from the good and the bad of our daily experimentation and passing on this knowledge to others or our future selves via feedback loops can only speed up the process of normalizing sustainability.

As an example, in the construction industry one of the major issues is that projects are often complex and involve a large number of players (in some commercial projects I worked on, more than 100 companies were involved, from master planning designers to tile fitters and everything in between). In projects like these, where people come and go over the years that they take from start to finish, it's hard to capture the lessons learned. Some teams do that, but it's rare that, on handing over the project to the client, there is a final meeting with every team that has worked on the project to share knowledge and learning.

Another issue is that designers and engineers rarely go back to a building after a few years to check whether it is performing as intended – and when it isn't, this phenomenon is commonly known as the *performance gap.*[104] This is a massive shame because often innovation doesn't have an opportunity to evolve and mature, as ingenious solutions (or warnings about bad mistakes!) are not passed onto the next project.

Given the characteristic experimental nature of sustainability, feedback loops should be planned from the start and implemented in every project. But how can we make it as effortless and systematized a process as possible so that it doesn't get overlooked?

Think about implementing automated ways of storing information for later retrieval and analysis: reports, emails and meeting minutes are a starting point, but consider how to capture *any* reflection on the key decisions taken in a project, as this is all valid information to learn from. AI summaries and transcripts offered by online meeting platforms like Zoom and Teams can be great tools to do this easily. Consider creating a database to collect all information and inputs as you go.

Once the information is gathered, the project team needs to analyse it. Think about how, when and who will be involved in this stage, and how to make sure key people put time aside to do it, better if in a co-creative environment.

Some decisions based on the insights gained from the analysis stage will need to be taken, and any relevant feedback will need to be distributed to all relevant stakeholders.

Finally, the necessary changes will need to be made.

In single conversations, feedback loops also have a place. Ask yourself and the other participants where possible:

How did the conversation go?

What could have been done differently?

What are the next steps?

---

[104] The performance gap is a major issue in sustainable design, and very difficult to pinpoint as it can depend on an enormous number of variables, from the way things are designed, to the choice of materials and technologies, to the way they are installed, to the way they are used. UK Green Building Council (2023, January 13). *Delivering Building Performance*. https://ukgbc.org/resources/delivering-building-performance/

This will be part of learning from each interaction and honing the art of communicating sustainability.

If you are keen to improve your communication style quickly, I suggest you keep a journal of your conversations for a month, ask yourself those three questions and review the answers on a weekly basis.

Step 4: Busting barriers

In Step 3, you have learned how to co-create solutions with others. But the reality is that sometimes, people are not keen to collaborate, let alone co-create. So in this step we will look at potential barriers to achieving the outcomes you hope for your conversations and sustainability communication.

As mentioned earlier, your job as a good communicator is to remove the barriers that are between you and the person you are speaking with, as opposed to pushing expert advice down their throats.

Some of the barriers will be in you, and some in the person in front of you.

Your communication style

I have talked about your mindset as a major barrier and the needed starting point for you to transform into a good communicator. Being open to connecting with others as opposed to fighting them is the first step towards a more fruitful relationship. But there is more.

Your attitude, and spoken and body language might be failing you. The way we speak and behave is a direct reflection of the way we feel, which is hard to mask. If you feel intimidated by a boardroom full of senior executives, it's hard not to show it in your demure or closed posture, your shaky tone of voice or your choice of words.

Language

We learn to use language that is complex in length and structure, jargon and technical terms, because we want to demonstrate that we know what we are talking about. Here are a few examples.

- Technical terminology (e.g. carbon token; circular economy; regeneration; closed-loop, greenwashing; materiality assessment; Scope 1, 2 and 3;[105] Net Zero; triple bottom line).

- Acronyms (e.g. ESG, TCFD, IPCC, SBTi, CSR, LCA, COP, GRI, SDGs, ISSB, BREEAM, LEED).[106]

- Long, convoluted sentences that look impressive on paper but sound clunky when said out loud.

Like anybody else, we want to maintain our *Status* when we are with our peers and with people we don't know. In situations in which we feel this *Status* is threatened (for instance, when we don't feel confident in front of clients), we tend to display our colourful feathers and use all the jargon we know to impress others and demonstrate that we do know our stuff.

Although understandable, this is not conducive to connecting to others' wavelengths. In fact, it creates a barrier that is hard to knock down, especially because language becomes part of who we are and we are rarely conscious of it. Your audience might be highly educated but in

[105] The Carbon Trust explains that the Greenhouse Gas Protocol – which provides the most widely recognized accounting standards for greenhouse gas emissions – categorizes GHG emissions into three 'scopes'. Scope 1 covers the direct emissions from owned or controlled sources. Scope 2 covers indirect emissions from the purchase and use of electricity, steam, heating and cooling. By using the energy, an organization is indirectly responsible for the release of these GHG emissions. Scope 3 includes all other indirect emissions that occur in the upstream and downstream activities of an organization, like purchased goods and services, business travel, waste disposal, use of sold products, etc. *What are Scope 3 emissions and why do they matter?* (2024, March 1). The Carbon Trust. www.carbontrust.com/our-work-and-impact/guides-reports-and-tools/what-are-scope-3-emissions-and-why-do-they-matter
[106] Environmental Social and Governance (ESG); Task Force on Climate Related Financial Disclosures (TCFD); Intergovernmental Panel on Climate Change (IPCC); Science-Based Targets initiative (SBTi); Corporate Social Responsibility (CSR); Life Cycle Assessment (LCA); Conference of the Parties (COP); Global Reporting Initiative (GRI); Sustainable Development Goals (SDGs); International Sustainability Standards Board (ISSB); BRE Environmental Assessment Method (BREEAM); Leadership in Energy and Environmental Design (LEED).

a different field; they might be highly experienced without having a degree; they might be young, or foreign and the language you speak might be their second language; they might be linguistically impaired. In each of these instances, using jargon or complex language will make your audience feel "less than" because they simply don't understand you. This will trigger their own *Status* threat alert, and they might not ask for clarification, so the gap between you and them widens.

Simplifying sustainability: how jargon-free language builds trust

Charlie C is the founder of a carbon footprint consultancy company.

Our company focuses on measuring and reducing our clients' carbon footprint and given the technical nature of what we do, I used to go all geeky with my first few clients.

I realized very quickly that this approach wasn't cutting it and that my language needed to be more accessible to form and maintain a long-term relationship with our clients. So I learned to clean my language of jargon.

For instance, talking about Scope 3 emissions I now just say that this is the carbon footprint of the client's supply chain. They don't need to get bogged down in the details, as it can be off putting and confusing, and we could lose their trust.

We invest a lot of time explaining our processes in simple terms and supporting our clients, but the advantage is that clients grow in understanding, and trust in the process and in our company – which means they are more likely to stick with us.

Here are a few ideas on how to jargon-proof your language and make your message crystal clear.

Have in mind your audience before a meeting. Ask yourself:

Would they understand the key concept of my work/proposition/idea?

Do I normally use words that my mum/80-year-old auntie/five-year-old nephew won't understand?

Here is an exercise that immediately changes people's perspective. In fact, stop reading and do it now!

Do your best to explain the core message of an idea or project you are working on to the rubber duck next to your screen as if it were someone who is not familiar with your work. If you catch yourself using any of the terminology above, try and rephrase it using plain language.

When you are in front of someone new, if you have done all the work until this point, you should know how to work out their level of understanding, and tailor your language accordingly. If you are in front of a large audience and know little about them, experiment with making your message as simple as possible as if you were a great orator speaking to the masses.

I invite you to study Winston Churchill delivering his famous *Their Finest Hour* 1940 speech to the nation bracing itself for a full attack.[107] Notice how Churchill (who later won the Nobel Prize in Literature for his speeches) slowly delivers his speech in short words and elegant, evocative metaphors. Yet he doesn't come across as trivial or like he doesn't know what he's talking about.

What can you learn from that, and how can it translate into your speeches and presentations?

Simple doesn't mean trivial. You don't want to come across as patronizing so ensure someone else listens to your speech before you deliver it officially, to make sure it's pitched at the right level.

If something is difficult to explain in spoken language, use other media: a sketch, a photograph or a diagram can sometimes be great crutches to support your delivery. Beware of using confusing graphs with too much data on, as you might obtain the opposite effect.

---

[107] Winston Churchill speech: Their Finest Hour (1940).

Think about delivering meaning before details.

> Imagine you have a glass jar. When you explain what's in it for them and the *big picture* first, this will be the mental container your audience will be able to fit the details into.

> Then imagine putting three large pebbles in it. These will be the three (no more, or your audience will easily forget) *key takeaways* from your speech or presentation.

> Finally, add some gravel, the *details* of your speech – only if the audience needs them, since the jar will be already pretty full.

Without the wider container, your audience will get lost in the details and won't know how to make sense of them. Without the pebbles, they won't understand the main takeaways from your argumentation.

Every time you prepare to have an important meeting or presentation, force yourself to stick to this rough structure by always remembering to take into consideration your audience's perspective first.

Use relatable metaphors from other fields, even from everyday life. Once I asked on LinkedIn what it feels like to be a sustainability leader battling with their everyday challenges. One contact replied that for them it's a crazy dance in which you start alone and initially look like a fool but then, when others join, they legitimize you as a leader and encourage more people to join, creating momentum and ultimately a movement. Her comment captured perfectly the grit and challenges that this role entails.

Ask your own clients or contacts to share with you a metaphor that explains the way they feel about sustainability. When you use their words in your future conversations, they are going to sound so much more relatable than what you can come up with as an outsider to their brain, and your audience will think that you have read their minds.

Delivery

The way you speak is as important, if not more important, than what you say. This goes even deeper than the words you choose, as mostly we are unaware of the way we speak – although video calls have helped us in the last few years to look at ourselves when we talk in meetings.

Human beings are inherently wired to pick up body language clues.[108]

It isn't an exact science but the general gist is that *closed postures* (rounded shoulders, not looking people in the eye) communicate that you want to close yourself like a hedgehog, you feel insecure, and are not ready to establish a rapport with your audience. They are also perceived as a sign of submission and perceived inferiority.

Open postures, on the other hand (shoulders back, open leg stance, relaxed smile, looking people in the eye) signal a willingness to connect but also of self-assurance (think about politicians and how they assume a "power pose" in their public appearances).

These behaviours are often instinctive and hard to change. My suggestion is to practise an open posture as much as possible when you are not seen and to remind yourself of it when you meet others.

If I had to choose one thing to always remember to do though, it would be to smile, genuinely, from the eyes – as this is the most important sign that you want to connect with others. If it is difficult because you feel poorly, had a bad day, month or year, or you are not a natural smiler, you can visualize happy memories from the past before your interaction. Try to feel the warm feeling of childhood holidays, the most special day of your life so far or think about someone you love dearly and who makes you laugh. It should make it easier to smile genuinely.

What about the pace and timbre of what you are delivering? When I first arrived in the UK many moons ago, I spoke really fast because I was incredibly conscious of my broken English. I instinctively thought that if I spoke fast, no one would focus on the many mistakes I was making.

Some of us just speak fast – I generally do – so it might take an additional effort to consciously slow down for the sake of making ourselves understood and to come across as more knowledgeable and charismatic.

---

[108] With some exceptions: for instance, some neurodivergent folks struggle with that.

It took some negative feedback on one of the first courses I ever delivered in English, and many years of practice while training people, for me to master the art of slowing down. I also learned not to fill the pauses with "uhms" and "eeers".

> Nothing strengthens authority so much as silence.
>
> *Leonardo da Vinci*

Again, Winston Churchill comes to our rescue here. Just notice how considerate each word and pause are in his speech. If you want a more recent example to look at, Barack Obama's 2008 presidential election night speech[109] is an example of mastery in oratory. Unlike Churchill, Obama also injects the emotional power of personal stories in his speech, including the story of a 106-year-old black woman from Atlanta. He takes the crowd on a journey to see this moment in history through her eyes.

Notice also how these people speak at a volume that can be heard without a microphone and modulate their voice to provide emphasis where it's needed the most.

If politicians are not your jam, stand-up comedians are the best next thing.

The expression "stand-up" is misleading, as these artists prepare their performances thoroughly and painstakingly. The use of carefully rehearsed and crafted pauses, modulation in their voice, emphasis on some words and facial expressions are more important than the actual words they use. But they also know how to roll with the punches. As we have seen in Step 3 of the framework, comedians use the *Yes… and* technique to quickly adapt their script to unexpected inputs from the audience.

Next time you watch a comedy show, pay attention to the delivery and see whether you can pick some elements you can practise in your everyday business life.

What can you learn from all these different styles of delivery?

How can you change the way you speak to communicate authority, interest and openness?

---

[109] CNN. (2012, November 7). *Raw Video: Barack Obama's 2008 acceptance speech* [Video]. YouTube. www.youtube.com/watch?v=LEo7lzfpdCU

Storytelling

I can't talk about your communication style without adding another little nudge to storytelling.[110] We have talked about using case studies as your hook to your audience, but here I want to talk about a simple and effective way to put this into practice.

Since writing *SustainABLE*, I have been a fan of Randy Olson's ABT (*And – But – Therefore*) technique. Olson, a scientist-turned-filmmaker, realized that brilliant scientific discoveries are often ignored by the general public because scientists are not great at communicating them. They generally use a flat AAA (*And – And – And*) structure to share fact, after fact, after fact.

This monotonous and sleep-inducing way of delivering science contributes to their failure to communicate sustainability to the world. Others start their speeches and never end anywhere. These speeches tend to be convoluted and do not have a clear structure. Olson calls them DHY (*Despite – However – Yet*).

To inject new life and interest into any presentation, even the driest carbon accounting report, Olson says:

> I call it the rule of replacing And's with either But's or Therefore... this happens, THEREFORE this happens, BUT this happens.

In other words, you need to start from the background to introduce the topic in context (*And*). Then, you need to add the *twist*, the challenge that the hero of the story (Your client? Yvon Chouinard, the Founder of Patagonia, giving his company away to environmental causes? Anita Roddick, founder of the Body Shop, starting an animal-cruelty-free beauty product shop in Brighton in the 1970s?) faced. That's the *But*. The more challenges the better for entertainment and interest purposes, of course.

---

[110] If you want a more in-depth step-by-step guide on sustainability storytelling, check out my previous book *SustainABLE* (2020).

Finally, how did the hero resolve the conflict or challenge? What did they do that can also be the lesson learned or the takeaway for your audience? That's your *Therefore*.

Analyse the case studies you normally use. Which structure do they follow?

Then have a go at using the ABT structure in your case studies and anecdotes. Write them down and practise with your rubber duck before trying them on a real audience, then notice the difference.[111]

Your audience's "unpersuadable" personality traits

As a sustainability leader, I'm pretty sure you have come across some people who just seem unpersuadable.[112] No matter how much proof you throw at them, they just won't budge. But... we also know that there can be cracks in the granite and people act against their main personality make-up now and then: bossy managers who occasionally show their soft side, selfish colleagues who are team players in an emergency and so on. Different situations can have a significant impact on people's behaviours.

As with anything to do with communication, you need to tune in with your inner badger and dig deep to find out in which situations the other person seems more prone to change their mind.

To help you with this, let's look at the four main character traits that can be a barrier when communicating (and influencing others on) sustainability.

---

[111] If you want to play a bit with this structure, you can challenge your colleagues to a game of storytelling on my website. You can roll some virtual dice that give you the three structures and some topics at random (everyday life as well as some sustainability ones). Green Gorilla UK | ABT Game (n.d.). www.thegreengorilla.co.uk/resources/abt-game

[112] Grant, A. (2021, March–April). Persuading the unpersuadable. *Harvard Business Review*.

Trait 1: Overconfidence

We all have to deal with arrogant people at times, which can be incredibly frustrating, as they seem to know it all. They cannot tolerate their *Status* being threatened by someone else's expertise.

If you have young children, you might be familiar with the cartoon Peppa Pig. Daddy Pig – Peppa's father – in every episode declares to be "an expert" in whatever situation is in, from making pizza to reading maps to putting pictures on a wall. Of course, he always turns out to be the opposite of that when it comes to showing his expertise. It's only when you put these Daddy Pigs in front of the challenge, and ask them to explain the process, that they fail to do so.

When you have to deal with an arrogant person, it would not work to point out their ignorance, because you'd only get a pushback. Remember, for every action, there is an opposite and equal reaction. A better way to persuade them is to *put them in front* of their ignorance – for instance, by asking them to explain their idea in detail. That's your opportunity to highlight the gaps that will open up in the process. And if they turn out to be right… Well, that's great! But if you don't check what they have in mind you will never know.

Trait 2: Stubbornness

Science demonstrated that stubborn people tend to value *Certainty* and consistency over other principles.[113] They believe that control over situations is determined by internal factors, as opposed to external circumstances. So when they make up their mind, these people can't be persuaded to change their opinion very easily. This means that if you present them a nicely packaged, fully formed solution, it doesn't matter how brilliant it is, it will get rejected.

---

[113] In the 1970s, in a seminal research study, West Virginia University's psychologists explored beliefs about control in a group of students. They examined whether individuals attributed success and failure to internal factors like effort or external factors like luck. Stubborn individuals tended to believe in internal control, seeing outcomes as subject to their own will. Biondo, J. and MacDonald, A. P. Jr. (1971). Internal-external locus of control and response to influence attempts. *Journal of Personality*, 39, 407–419.

The best way forward with stubborn people is to plant a seed so that it can grow in their minds. Asking questions that start with *"What if… ?"* and *"Could we… ?"* instead of giving answers can be a winning strategy here, as you give back the control they need by inviting them to share their thoughts and start imagining possibilities. Additionally, since they will feel involved, they might be more prone to shift perspective and be persuaded to give that little seed more consideration.

Co-creation here is, once again, the way forward.

Trait 3: Narcissism

In my life, I had to deal with two narcissistic people very close to me. They would say things like: "I don't admire anyone because no one is better than me." Or if they had an argument at work, they'd always think everyone else was wrong, never them.

Once, one of them told me: "I saw Life's Truth, so I can't be wrong." (I have to be honest, I was so stunned by this statement, that I didn't ask what sort of "Saint Paul on the Road to Damascus" illumination they had… but you get the gist.)

You have probably experienced yourself how difficult it is to convince a narcissist of something. One could reasonably think that narcissists have solid self-esteem when, in fact, research[114] demonstrates that their self-esteem is actually unstable. Narcissists have a rather fragile ego, crave *Status* and approval, and feel threatened when they are criticized. However, depending on the situation, they can demonstrate humility… when their ego is massaged a bit.

Crucially, praising a narcissist for the same thing you are trying to persuade them of is a pointless exercise. For instance, if you believe your CEO made a mistake in not incorporating sustainability deeply enough when they formulated the company's strategy, it would be pointless to praise their strategic minds. Think about what you *genuinely* admire about that person (there must be something there!). Is it their

[114] Baumeister, R. F., Bushman, B. J. and Campbell, W. K. (2000). *Self-Esteem, Narcissism, and Aggression. Current Directions in Psychological Science.*

resilience in times of crisis? Is it their integrity? Because both can be useful traits in sustainability. For instance, you could say:

> *I really admire how you kept the ship from sinking during the pandemic with integrity and resilience. I believe integrating sustainability into our strategy can only build on your efforts and make us more resilient should something like this happen again.*

We are not as monolithic as we think; we all have a range of personalities and praising one of them will make that person more open to accepting suggestions or that they have shortcomings elsewhere.

Trait 4: Disagreeableness

Disagreeable people are argumentative and competitive. Separating the person from the issue will help because you'll need to demonstrate assertiveness without engaging in a cock fight, and come back again and again to this person with new ideas and fresh perspectives instead, until you find the right input they will latch onto. This is where developing your resilience will support your work in sustainability.

Don't take a "no" as a final answer. If you are convinced that your idea is the right one for you, your audience and the Planet, then think of it as a "no for now" and as a stimulus to refine the issue and find novel ways to address it. If you are time-poor, you might want to have a range of inputs ready for the disagreeable person to mull over instead of offering fully fleshed-out ideas you may invest a lot of time in only to be rejected.

Remember that these people love to argue, and if you know how to argue back and stand up for yourself without taking it personally, you might even earn their respect!

Common barriers to SHIFTing behaviours

There are many reasons, besides personalities, that can trigger the negative reactions of your audience when you try to persuade them to adopt sustainability. You'll see how they are also connected with the five SCARF domains that determine our social interactions. To help memorize them, think that they can be listed under the acronym

SHIFT:[115] *Social influence, Habits, Individual self, Feelings and cognition,* and *Tangibility.* Let's look at them one by one.

Social influence

As we have seen, we are social beings, and this is what often determines our seemingly irrational behaviours. In business, we think market norms determine everything (think about that consultant who was puzzled when he presented well thought through financial benefits of sustainability to his colleagues and got rejected). The reality is, we also have very strong social norms that make us human.

We compare ourselves to others all the time. That's why social media started as a great way of connecting people who are physically far from each other but can often end up making us outright miserable as we compare our lives with the seemingly perfect lives (and businesses) of others.

How can we use the social influence people feel so strongly about to make them shift their perspective on sustainability? You need to appeal to different personality types (think about the DISC traits – *Dominant, Influential, Steady* or *Compliant*; see Figure 3) and provide for each their own social proof that sustainability is not only a nice to have but a necessity.

- With big vision people in general and *Influential* people in particular, showcase how others have successfully adopted sustainability. Put together some strong case studies that resonate directly with them.

- Show *Influential* people how they can get ahead of others by being more sustainable; highlight how they can showcase their sustainable behaviours publicly to promote their business, and attract new and better customers and talent.

- With *Compliant* and *Dominant* people, prepare some solid data that demonstrate your argument based on other people's experience

---

[115] These reflections have been developed starting from the work done by White, K., Habib, R., and Hardisty, D. J. (2019). How to SHIFT consumer behaviours to be more sustainable: A literature review and guiding framework. *Journal of Marketing,* 83(3), 22–49.

(with fewer details and more straight-to-the-point conclusions for the latter).

- With *Compliant* and *Steady* people, be ready to answer all the risk-related questions looking at how others have dealt with similar challenges before.

- With *Dominant* people, highlight their shared sustainable identity with other successful and high-status people.

Habits

We have survived millennia of hardship and evolution by automating many of our repeated habits to save our mental energies for novel challenges. This means that once a behaviour becomes a habit (from purchasing goods to waste disposal) it is extremely hard to break that established mental pattern and introduce a different one. It feels safe to keep doing the same thing, even if in the long run it is detrimental to the business or ourselves.

It's easy to keep on purchasing from the same supplier we have been using for years because we know their products, even if they are not the most sustainable, or to bank with the same bank which we know invests in fossil fuels, but somehow it feels so hard to switch from.

Sometimes we put up with price increases or lowering of quality because it requires mental energy to switch to another provider. But are these products the right ones in the face of a changing climate or a scaling business? Are they responding to the new challenge posed by more stringent legislation, or Diversity and Inclusion pressures?

When people are stuck in a rut of habit, you can try some of these techniques.

- Highlight the difficulty of carrying on as usual (e.g. finding insurance coverage for an unsustainable business).

- Highlight the potential penalties (e.g. taxes, fines, higher prices) if the unsustainable behaviour continues (e.g. discharging chemicals in the watercourses because the old filters do not capture them).

- Encourage your audience to "just try" the new sustainable behaviour or product (e.g. one new product line, or a new weekly check on the machinery to ensure it works as expected). Perhaps you can present it as a limited time experiment to lower their resistance to change.

- Highlight the advantages of the new behaviour (e.g. the ease of use, time and money saving – for instance, new electronic technology that detects leaks automatically as opposed to visual checks) and incentives (e.g. grants, rebates, tax relief schemes).

- Automate the new behaviour as much as possible so that decisions need to be taken only once (e.g. direct debits and automatic renewals of contracts; software instead of manual calculations).

- Help your audience by lowering uncertainty and friction in the switch to sustainability (e.g. by providing templates, explanations, training, prompts and so on).

Individual self

Individuals want to reinforce a positive self-view and can become defensive when they learn that their own behaviours are causing a negative impact. Change can feel like a threat to the identity of the individual. For instance, conservatives might not engage with progressive sustainable behaviour for fear of losing their identity or the respect of their closed circle.

- Highlight the positive associations of sustainable behaviours with the self (e.g. by accentuating the alignment with their individual and/or company values).

- If you are struggling with promises that do not get fulfilled, a written commitment can increase the likelihood that your audience will engage in sustainable behaviour, as it will reinforce their identity as people who keep their promises (who likes to identify with the unreliable type?).

- Highlight how they might be already engaging in sustainable behaviours in other parts of their lives: consistency reinforces self-identity.

- Describe the positive outcomes and impacts of sustainable behaviour to reinforce its importance and meaning.

- Stress the big picture's benefits; many people want to be part of something bigger than themselves.

- At the same time, what's in it for them as individuals (e.g. *Status*, glory, publicity, more money, a promotion)?

Feelings and cognition

People behave according to either what they know or what they feel, or a combination of the two. We have talked about how we need to avoid leading with our values as they can trigger negative feelings if the values are misaligned or if the audience feels like their *Status* is under threat. So, what can you do to avoid putting up barriers?

- Whenever possible, aim at provoking positive emotions (that "warm glow" feeling of having a positive impact). Perhaps show people how their contribution will *directly* benefit the community they live and work in? I love going into schools as an ambassador of my local sustainability charity and telling children about what is in their power to do to keep our Planet healthy and beautiful.

- Avoid provoking strong negative emotions (e.g. shame, fear, sadness) as they can paralyse the person to inaction. This is when negative messaging about climate change becomes overwhelming, causing people to freeze instead of sprinting to action.

- Saying that, showing people what they'll lose by not adopting sustainable behaviours will be more effective than showing them what they'll gain. We all suffer from *loss aversion bias*.

- Show urgency and relevance to the individual.[116] How is the behaviour of the person in front of you going to affect them and their immediate circle and surroundings? Or perhaps the places

---

[116] Polar bears, as much as they are cute on Christmas cards, are too distant from the ordinary lives of most people to change their behaviour, unless your audience is made of six-year-old children. Generally speaking, children feel a lot more connected to Nature and are more sensitive to harm to animals than adults as their sense of wonder for the natural world is still alive.

where they grew up? A fellow sustainability professional once told me that she pivoted her job towards sustainability a few years ago because, as a keen skier, she was heartbroken to witness the French Alps seeing less and less snowfall over the years.

- Simple, clear messaging that shows causes, effects and impacts can affect behavioural change, however not in isolation. You'll need to combine this with other tactics – as the world of advertisement teaches us. Let's look at what factors determine advertising campaigns' success.

  - *When* the ads are shown to people: most charities send on-air donation campaigns around Christmas because people feel more generous and altruistic then. In your sustainability work, that means choosing carefully when to present your ideas to your audience depending on their mental space and circumstances.

  - How much ads encourage people to question their own behaviours and expose *incongruencies* between their perceived and true self.

  - *How relatable* they are: it's more likely you'll donate to a multiple sclerosis charity having seen an ad if you or someone close to you suffers from it. What emotional angle of your argument can your audience relate to?

  - *How many times* you are exposed to an ad: in an increasingly noisy world we get bombarded by thousands of messages every day. Persistence is key to getting noticed: this is why you keep on seeing the same ads across different digital platforms. Marketeers know that there is an *effective frequency*, i.e. how many times you need to be exposed to a message before you become curious and engage with it (on average, between three and 11).[117]

In your sustainability work, you'll need to refine your message and persistently share it, from different perspectives if needed, until it strikes an emotional chord with your audience.

[117] Team, M. S. (2023, October 6). *Effective Frequency – Definition & Meaning. MBA Skool.* www.mbaskool.com/business-concepts/marketing-and-strategy-terms/13155-%20 effective-frequency.html

Tangibility

In Part 1 of this book we talked about the fact that the climate crisis and its associated issues don't "have a face", they usually don't present an immediate threat to life as we know it, but they are rather a silent killer sneaking in. That's the reason why, especially in reactive businesses where firefighting is the norm, sustainability is not seen as a priority. If this is the case with your audience, what can you do?

- You can show them the immediate, concrete effects of unsustainable *and* sustainable behaviours, close to the interests of the individual or company: e.g. how the changing climate is already affecting their supply chain or staff wellbeing in the hotter months; when it looks like climate change is affecting only far away countries, you can refer to the local warming climate via Dr Ed Hawkins' Climate Stripes in the company's area[118] and its effects, like the massive increase in fish mass death due to water pollution and warmer UK watercourses, widely reported in recent years' news; or you can show potential improvements in the local community.

- Lack of *Certainty* leads to greenwashing and inaction. Focus on proven facts and benefits around sustainable behaviour, especially if you are dealing with *Dominant* or *Compliant* people.

- Highlight the risk management advantages of a sustainable business.

Reframing sustainability: aligning sustainability goals with business priorities

Conor M is a Senior Carbon Management Consultant for a leading sustainability consultancy.

During my 15 years in the sustainability industry, I've seen a dramatic shift in attitudes, particularly in the construction sector. Initially, setting Net Zero targets, especially including Scope 3 emissions, was met with scepticism. Now it's a

---

[118] https://showyourstripes.info/

standard for major contractors, indicating a broad acceptance and commitment to sustainability across the industry. My conversations have evolved from justifying sustainability to strategizing its implementation. Despite this progress, in large organizations there's a persistent challenge at the project delivery level due to high pressures on programme and cost, where sustainability is still often viewed as an additional expense or programme delay factor rather than a business benefit.

To address this, sustainability professionals need to adopt a more commercial approach: by aligning sustainability initiatives with business priorities – such as cost savings, programme efficiency, and client satisfaction – we can reframe sustainability as an integral part of operational success rather than a peripheral concern.

For instance, when we worked with the UK Ministry of Defence, they were more receptive to sustainability when it was framed as operational resilience rather than environmental benefits, e.g. using solar panels to reduce the reliance on risky fuel supplies in remote areas. Additionally, effective sustainability requires collaboration and co-creation across teams, including design, commercial and procurement. Sustainability professionals can achieve this by providing practical steps and training to show how sustainability can be integrated into existing processes. This approach not only reduces resistance but also promotes a more inclusive and effective implementation of sustainability initiatives.

Cognitive biases

Another major barrier to the sustainability message getting through is a type of "mental shortcut" that affects everybody, including sustainability leaders and professionals: *cognitive biases*. Encyclopaedia Britannica defines them as:

> Systematic errors in the way individuals reason about the world due to subjective perception of reality. Cognitive biases are predictable patterns of error in how the human brain functions and therefore are widespread.[119]

The interesting fact about cognitive biases is that, although they can lead to errors, they are in fact an advantage of human evolution. Our brains, bombarded daily with thousands of information inputs, create shortcuts to save energy when elaborating some of the data by labelling them quickly, generalizing and stereotyping.

One prominent framework to understand human decision-making is the two-system model proposed by psychologist and Nobel Prize for Economics Daniel Kahneman.[120] This model outlines two distinct systems of thought that operate concurrently, each serving different purposes:

- **System 1** represents rapid, automatic cognition to handle routine observations and unconscious information processing. Decisions made under this system often occur effortlessly, without conscious deliberation.

- **System 2,** in contrast, denotes deliberate, conscious thinking that can override System 1 but requires time and effort to engage. While System 1 processing can introduce cognitive biases and influence our decisions, employing careful System 2 reasoning can help identify and rectify these biases through self-reflection.

Cognitive biases affect everyone, even the most rational of individuals, and they can be a real issue when dealing with sustainability. By establishing a rapport with your audience before you work with them, you'll have an opportunity to uncover any potential biases they might have, so it's worth being aware of a few common ones that could stop people from engaging fully with what you are saying. Here they are…

---

[119] Eldridge, S. (2023, March 10). Cognitive bias. *Encyclopedia Britannica.* www.britannica.com/science/cognitive-bias
[120] Kahneman, D. (2011). *Thinking, Fast and Slow.*

Confirmation bias

Have you noticed how we tend to listen only to information that confirms our preconceptions and unconsciously look for proof that our worldview is "the right one"? You can see this for yourself in an online search, in your social media feed and in your LinkedIn connections. We tend to listen and get closer to people and opinions we agree with. Very rarely do we open up to a different voice that goes against what we already believe in.

Similarly, if the people you speak with don't already have sustainability as a core belief (or, worse, they think it's a fad) they will not have the opportunity to hear about it as much as they hear about finance, lifestyle, fashion, sport or whatever else they care about.

Of course, once these two worlds collide in a meeting, they'll be just as shocked as you about your views. And you'll be labelled as an opponent. Pretty much this whole book is about becoming curious about others, which means getting underneath the skin of our own and our audience's confirmation bias.

Giving ourselves time to self-reflect and keep track of our conversations; being open to listening to people from different backgrounds and beliefs; gathering information from different sources; asking questions and adopting a systems thinking approach will help cast light on the areas in which our audience and us might have a bias.

Bandwagon effect

The probability of one person adopting a belief increases based on the number of people who hold that belief; and when that person will seek more proof of that belief because of *confirmation bias*, they will find it. We have covered how we seek social proof and are influenced by what others are doing or thinking.

We can use this bias to our advantage though, as we offer social proof that confirms *our* ideas to our audience – this can take the form of case studies, and showing their competitors' sustainability journey and positive results. The bandwagon effect also means that if you manage to find common ground with them through the process explained in

Step 1 of the framework (e.g., by asking deep and open questions, and active listening), you'll be more likely to build trust, and they will be more likely to take into consideration your ideas.

Cognitive dissonance

This is about having inconsistent thoughts or beliefs, especially relating to behavioural decisions and attitude change. It is a massive one in sustainability. Because of the complexity of this field, and how much unsustainable attitudes are ingrained in our society, it is hard to be consistent across all aspects of our businesses and lives. For example, we know flying is one of the major aggravators to the climate emergency, yet many of us keep using a plane for holidays or work. Or perhaps we might be doing something because of convenience or habit even though we know it isn't the most sustainable choice (shopping from a certain online store, eating certain foods, driving a certain car...). But it doesn't feel completely good, or guilt-free.

These conflicting thoughts and behaviours can cause anxiety and other negative feelings, and can be triggered by social pressure. Cognitive dissonance can present itself if the person you are speaking with in principle agrees with you but their actions are inconsistent with their beliefs. What to do then?

Because often we do it without realizing, one way of addressing cognitive dissonance is to highlight it. Having done the work to build rapport with your audience and get to know them, it will be easier for you to spot any contradiction. You can tactfully point out to the person you are speaking with that they have said they wanted to embrace sustainability yet they are not acting to make it happen. Then perhaps offer to help them go from thoughts to action. Biases are hard to eliminate, so offering to take some of that burden away might do the trick.

If you are affected by cognitive dissonance, mindfulness and being curious about your own thoughts and behaviours is a great first step towards overcoming it.

Conservatism bias, status quo bias and loss aversion bias

These biases show up in people who are comfortable in the current state of affairs, often people who have been working in a certain industry for a while, and value it more than what they could have, even when changing is more advantageous.

When I was working in construction, I used to hear all the time people saying things like: "Why change the way we have been building in the last thirty years if it works? Sustainability is a passing trend." But often, keeping things as they are means we will lose out long-term – like in the case of holding on to inefficient systems just because we are used to them.

Because people need at least twice as good a deal to switch to something different,[121] if you want to have a shot at changing someone's behaviour, you'll need to demonstrate double the benefits of sustainability compared to the status quo. A couple of powerful questions you might ask your audience if they have a status quo, loss aversion or conservatism bias are:

What happens if you do nothing?

What doing nothing cost you?

Curse of knowledge

This is for us sustainability folks: when people who are well-informed cannot understand the common man. Can we get down from our ivory tower and meet people who don't have the same knowledge as us?

As soon as you realize you might be suffering from this bias, put into practice all the work you have been doing so far – from grounding yourself to calming down and allowing your rational brain to take over from your "lizard brain"; to building rapport and being curious about the other person; to believing they are at least 10% right, and working towards co-creating solutions with them as opposed to lecturing them about sustainability.

---

[121] Novemsky, N., and Kahneman, D. (2005). The boundaries of loss aversion. *Journal of Marketing Research*, 42(2), 119–128.

Hyperbolic discounting

This is the tendency for people to want an immediate payoff rather than a larger gain later on, another common issue in sustainability. You can take advantage of this bias by spotting some quick wins as a consequence of adopting your ideas to hook your audience in. You know that once you have that "foot in the door", it will be easier to get your audience to open up more fully to sustainability.

Negativity bias

The tendency to put more emphasis on negative experiences rather than positive ones. Negativity bias helped us survive over millennia because we can envisage the worst case scenario and prepare for it, but it's not necessarily helping now, when we need all the hope and optimism we can muster to reverse the trends that threaten to destroy us. I'm not implying that we are *not* in a crisis, but if we focus on the negative, we'll feel disempowered to do anything about it because... what's the point?

This bias can also be found in our audience when they don't believe adopting sustainability is worth the effort. Can you show them some practical and tangible advantages of it without necessarily going into the ethical argument?[122]

Ostrich effect

The decision to ignore dangerous or negative information by "burying" our heads in the sand. This affects most people, who in the face of overwhelming situations, freeze and decide not to act.

A way out of this bias is to unpack overwhelming information and adopt a step-by-step approach as explained in Step 3 of the framework. You can also focus on the advantages to counterbalance some of the negatives as illustrated in the negativity bias section.

---

[122] A reminder that in Appendix C you'll find a full list of potential sustainability advantages that can work across sectors. Make sure you substantiate them with relevant case studies and data specific to your industry.

Tragedy of the commons

We overuse common resources because it's not in any individual's interest to conserve them. You hear people say it all the time: "It's not my fault or my responsibility. Why should I give up international air travel when the big corporations continue to pollute 10,000 times more than me?" Remember the old guy in my town saying his house was spotless while he chucked rubbish on the road because it was the council's responsibility to clean it up?

This is a hard one to overcome because in some cases, these people are right! One person jumping on a plane, one plastic bottle on the floor or one person eating meat do not change much. But it's the cumulative effect of our individual actions on several fronts, which reinforce and interact in complex ways, that causes the problems.

There is also another effect that individual actions can have, which is a lot more powerful than the actions themselves: the capacity to inspire others to do the same. Our individual ripple effect. It's a seed we plant that who knows what it will germinate into.

If your audience hides behind this bias to avoid doing the right thing, you can employ some of the techniques shared so far and talk about the advantages of sustainability as previously discussed.

How to prepare before the conversation

I have covered a large range of potential barriers you might encounter in your sustainability conversations, and I appreciate it can be quite overwhelming. I suggest you add to your pre-meeting preparation work some thinking time about how to pre-empt any objections or barriers, based on what you know about the people you are going to meet.

Some clues about potential biases and barriers will come from the analysis of the context as well as the background of the audience, as looked at in Steps 1 and 2:

- political, economic, social, technological, legal, environmental (PESTLE) context issues

- character traits (DISC)

- position in the company and responsibilities

- likely level of interest

- background (education level; years in the company; culture).

But be careful not to pigeon-hole people. If we go into a meeting with preconceptions about our audience based, for instance, on their ethnicity or education level, we are going to fall into the very trap we want to avoid without even realizing it: biases.

What we are trying to do here is to find out whether they *might* have any objections or biases as a consequence of those components, and prepare accordingly.

Ground yourself beforehand so that you are fully present and enter any such conversations with an open mind and with the hope of being pleasantly surprised: this is fundamental to having the right attitude and creating the strong rapport you need to co-create the conversation.

If you have identified potential biases you might want to pre-empt them during the meeting.

By putting the potential biases or objections on the table, you'll diffuse their power over the conversation. You can say something like:

> *You might be thinking that this is a step too far for your business* (status quo/conservatism bias), *which I have noticed takes pride in its traditional methods of manufacturing, however the solutions we are proposing will preserve your family business for years to come by innovating discreetly and increasing efficiency.*

Or

> *I know the economic scenario is quite challenging at the moment* (economic context), *indeed many of my clients are having issues with cash flow; however, I'm sure we can start from a like-for-like change in the materials without affecting your bottom line. In fact, by implementing these changes you'll start to see some savings straightaway.*

Or

> *I appreciate how your organization is focused on digital automation at the moment, just like others in the field, and I appreciate how you think your*

company is small and has a relatively minor impact on the environment (bandwagon effect/Influential personality/tragedy of the commons). *However, sustainability can enable this transformation in a way that future-proofs your business and if done at the same time as the other changes, it can be integrated smoothly into the new system, and set you apart from your competitors by enhancing your reputation as a sustainable provider.*

In any case, offer to involve them in the decisions as peers and co-create the outcomes as opposed to imposing your expertise: *Will you be open to exchange some ideas?*

While introducing the advantages of a different approach, you need to respect their views of their business, even if heavily biased, just like you would respect their status.

Remember to praise their work (especially if you are dealing with a narcissistic audience!), start small and build on any common ground or small opening they might give you.

Step 5: Commitment and way forward

Having built rapport with your audience, worked together to co-create goals and potential solutions, and overcome some barriers that could prevent sustainability from being adopted, the last step in this framework is about getting your audience to commit to change and continuous improvement.

Donald Sull, Management Professor and *Harvard Business Review* contributor, defines commitment in a business context as "an action taken in the present that binds an organization to a future course of action".[123] In everyday life, we know how hard it is to commit to something that will have an impact on our future actions, and stick to it: going to the gym, eating plant-based, reading and other things we know would be good for us. But why is it so hard?

If you have reached this point and overcome all the hurdles to get your audience to the point of being willing to embrace sustainability, it's important to understand how to go from words to facts. Because just having the *willingness* to change doesn't equate to *actual* change.

---

[123] Sull, D. (2003, June). Managing by commitments. *Harvard Business Review.*

Sustainability intentions vs. actions

The Theory of Planned Behaviour[124] is a psychological theory that links intentions to behaviour. This theory states that what you do depends on whether you have set an intention for it, what you think others will say about it, and whether you think you can actually do it.

So if you, for instance, were planning to adopt a plant-based diet, it has been demonstrated that being motivated and setting the intention to do it will give you more chances that you will act on that intention, but whether you actually go plant-based will depend also on what other people think. Again, we are social beings! Are your family/friends fans of massive meat barbecues and Sunday roasts and are they going to frown upon your new diet? Or are they also keen on switching? Plus, whether *you* think you can actually do it. Do you identify as someone who is disciplined and determined and can stick to their commitments? Or do you think it will be difficult to adopt a plant-based diet because of your lack of time for meal prep?

More recently, in a study concerning sustainable consumer behaviour, researchers have hypothesized that to determine whether people will be willing to act sustainably or not, more variables are needed.[125]

These are:

- being personally concerned about environmental or societal issues

- having an already established habit to act sustainably

- feeling obliged because of ethical or cultural reasons to act in a certain way

- believing that our actions will have an effect on the environment and society

- having enough knowledge and information about the impact of the individual's behaviour on the environment and society.

---

[124] Ajzen, I. (1991). The Theory of Planned Behaviour. *Organisational Behaviour and Human Decision Processes*, 50(2), 179–211.
[125] Hosta, M. and Zabkar, V. (2021, June). Antecedents of environmentally and socially responsible sustainable consumer behavior. *Journal of Business Ethics*, 171(2), 273–293.

Committing to sustainability in business

Although there are many more layers of control and rationalization when it comes to committing to something in business, companies are run by people, and for this reason, we can apply some of the theories above to the business environment.

For sustainability to be implemented, it's important therefore that your audience:

- has a strong intention to do it
- has colleagues, especially top management, who are firmly on board
- is confident in the plan to achieve their goals and the positive impacts on their business, society and the environment
- has a strong support system to make it happen
- has enough knowledge to carry out their sustainability commitments.

Hopefully, having gone through the five steps in this framework, by now all of these will be in place. If not, you can probe your audience with the following questions:

Do you have enough sustainability supporters and champions inside your team, especially at top management level?

What are your competitors doing in sustainability?

Do you believe you (and your teams) can implement sustainability as planned?

Do you have an operational system in place to help you reach your goals?

Who is doing what by when?

What framework do you have in place to review the commitments on a regular basis and ensure continuous improvement?

How do you communicate with your stakeholders?

Does the new system align with your existing mission and values? If not, what can be done to marry them up?

What (negative and positive) impacts do you think your actions will have on the environment and society, as well as on your profit targets?

Do you have enough sustainability knowledge and skills within the team? If not, do you need to hire new specialist resources or run training courses to fill any gap?

From words to action

One more thing needs to be done: building up the habit of doing things differently. That's where commitments come into play.

Commitments have the power to change the identity and culture of an organization, or simply to reinforce it. But commitments are a double-edged sword, as they crystalize the company's behaviour for the foreseeable future. And if conditions change, the company might find itself locked into an outdated path, with commitments becoming liabilities.[126] This is a very likely scenario in sustainability, the ever-evolving field. No wonder your audience might be nervous about committing to anything new.

So, what sort of commitment should you elicit from your audience?

Whether the company has expressed an intention to invest money and resources, divest from fossil fuels, pledge to achieve a specific goal, partner with others on a business venture, or implement new systems or strategies, committing to a first step in the right direction will provide an *anchor* on which the company can then pivot and build the habit of operating sustainability. This is especially useful if your audience is still resistant to embedding sustainability at a strategic level.

As explained in Step 2, starting small is a good way to lower the bar of resistance to change, gather wider consensus and allow the company to try the new direction while minimizing the risks they associate with it, a sort of Minimum Viable Product to test the new intentions, e.g., a single project, a limited-edition product or a temporary arrangement to allow people to get used to the new order gradually and to gather feedback and adjust accordingly.

---

[126] Sull, D. (2003, June). Managing by commitments. *Harvard Business Review.*

This anchor needs to be a modest but firm, innovative first step in a different direction that breaks with the past and proves that change is possible, but not so big that it triggers a negative reaction.

Once the anchor has been identified, in order to make it into a commitment, it needs to be simply and clearly defined, measurable and widely communicated, and have buy-in from all the key stakeholders involved (not just top management) so that it is credible.

The risk otherwise is that the anchor will be just another token created to placate investors or the public's demand. Everyone needs to believe in the new move, especially the key stakeholders who have power and influence over the project, as identified in Step 1.

Most of the leaders I spoke to had a similar experience when they were pushing their boards to buy into sustainability: they would present the same six slides over and over again until everyone, from graduates to senior management, knew by heart the key characteristics and, most importantly, the "why" of the new initiative. This is a necessary step to ensure the message lands and the culture of a company starts to shift and evolve towards a more sustainable outlook.

Still on the subject of credibility, it's also important, in line with Aristotle's predicament, that someone with kudos and authority within the company acts as the anchor's champion. The messenger is as important as the message here.

Once this first step has been taken, it is important to align it with the company's other frameworks, strategies, processes and, most importantly, values.

Values are the compass we follow to orient ourselves in life, and since companies are made of people, the new values must be aligned with the top managers' values and consistent with their ethos. If there is any misalignment, sustainability will never be a priority and the commitment will not be fulfilled. The bottom line is, managers and directors need to be on board for change to happen.

As explained in Step 4, it is possible to persuade the seemingly unpersuadable leaders but it takes persistent action by committed individuals who would have to build rapport overtime and be strategic about focusing their energy on the key stakeholders.

Finally, the company should review their progress, long-term goals and commitments on a regular basis, and ensure they are still relevant and aligned with their mission, vision and values (as well as against external demands, challenges and inputs). It would be a good idea to re-evaluate sustainability commitments and goals during planned management reviews, e.g. Annual General Meetings (AGM), with the aim to continuously improve and, eventually, integrate sustainability within the core mission of the organization.

Ensuring impact: KPIs and follow-through in climate awareness programmes

Sandra S, whom we've already met, is an event organizer and workshop facilitator.

I refuse to run climate awareness programmes within a company which hasn't laid out a plan of action after the programme. To avoid this situation, together with the client we usually agree on KPIs to measure how much more the employees understand the overall climate change challenge after the programme, then the overall engagement and direction taken by their company and, ultimately, if they would be willing to engage more actively internally (by becoming climate ambassadors, for example).

I usually talk simultaneously to the Sustainability and HR Departments to ensure the commitments to action will be followed up thoroughly by both departments.

What's next?

Congratulations!

You have reached the end of this book, but this is only the beginning of your bright future as a Good Communicator: a sustainability leader who can confidently convey one of the most important messages of our time, and make a real difference as a consequence.

By now, you have become *aware* of the fact that you want to change: you got this book, you read it, you reached the final chapter. Its content made you *think* about what you are already doing well when communicating sustainability and what you can do to improve your communication style.

Perhaps these thoughts generated some *feelings*, like frustration that your interactions with others might not have the impact you'd like yet, or a sense of anticipation for what you now know you can do to improve. When you feel strongly about something, it's a good indication that you have the drive to change.

As you might have experienced before, though, reading a book rarely changes the way you behave. Books are wonderful to generate insights and inspire. But it's *how you put into practice* the content and ideas from the book that can truly change your life.

From this point onwards, my friend, it's up to you.

This is where you need to start taking *action*.

First – as you'd want your clients to do – you need to *commit to change*. Think about what you would be losing by not investing time and energy into your sustainability communication (you see how all the techniques I covered in this book can be applied in your own life!).

Then, you need to create *systems* to help you automate decisions and make it easier for you to make the Good Communicator framework a *habit*. For instance, you could plan to use the framework and its tools in your next meeting, starting from a low-stakes one (perhaps an internal meeting with colleagues you already know).

Then you can plan at least one meeting a week in which you'll use the framework, until you are confident to use it in every interaction you have.

It's important to flag up these meetings in your calendar and add an hour of preparation time before them to start with – once you get familiar with the framework, your prep time will shorten but remember the famous quote commonly attributed to Abraham Lincoln:

> Give me six hours to chop down a tree and I will spend the first four sharpening the axe.

Preparation is a fundamental step to your success as a good communicator and should not be skipped.

Finally, remember to practise at every opportunity. The more you use the techniques, the more confident you'll become. Look for opportunities to engage in conversations, give presentations, or participate in discussions. Keep a journal of your interactions for a month so that you can learn from them and adjust your communication strategy accordingly.

Once the habit of communicating sustainability in this new way is established, true change will happen because then you *will be* a Good Communicator.

And if you still struggle to make it all a reality, remember to check out the bonus resources and help available at www.thegreengorilla.co.uk/the-good-communicator.

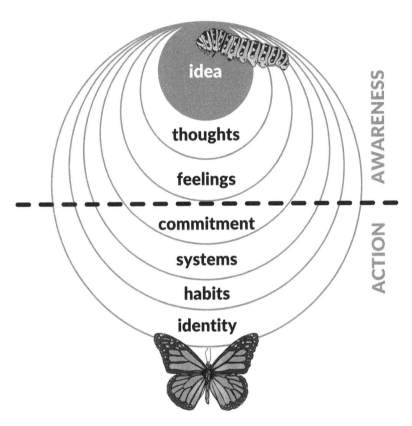

Figure 16 *How you will transform into a Good Communicator*

Appendix A: The Good Communicator: key steps and techniques

Before the meeting or presentation	Chapter
• Start by checking in on **your mindset**: your aim should be not to change someone's mind or to conduct a crusade against them, but to address the issue you will discuss with them. Get into the meeting with the spirit of co-creation.	Part 2: Shifting mindsets
• Slow down. Use the physiological sigh and focus on your senses to ground, calm your lizard brain down and activate your rational, neocortex brain. • Notice your body sensations as you go through this process and any negative emotions about the meeting, without judgement.	

• Choose the qualities you want to deploy to deal with the situation in a wiser way and choose consciously to go on a voyage of discovery of the people you'll meet.	
• Define the **scope of the communication**. • Why are you meeting or presenting to these people? Having a clear purpose for the meeting and a call to action at the end is key to having a productive interaction. • Would an email be a better way of communicating in this instance? • Where are you meeting them? Is there anything in the meeting environment that can get in the way of the communication?	Part 2: How to shift mindsets to communicate sustainability successfully – Why – Who – Where
• Think about the **people you will be meeting with**. • What are their likely mindsets and character traits? Do some research about your audience if this is the first time you meet them (similarly to market research profiling: their *demographics, behaviours, geographic and psychographic*). • Do you have anything in common that could be a conversation starter?	Part 2: How to shift mindsets to communicate sustainability successfully – Finding out what makes people tick
Think about their personalities, and try to identify whether they are *Dominant, Influential, Steady* or *Compliant* (**DISC**) from any communication and interaction you might have had so far.	Part 2: How to shift mindsets to communicate sustainability successfully – Who

• Think about what **arguments and communication style** would work best for each of the meeting attendees or audience as a whole – in line with their personalities, roles, background and interests. • Think about the **delivery of your message**. Organize your thoughts beforehand and focus on delivering your key message effectively by rehearsing. Learn how to speak to communicate authority, interest and openness from politicians and comedians.	Part 3 Step 4: Busting Barriers – Your communication style
• Some people seem **unpersuadable**. Depending on their personality traits (from overconfidence to stubbornness to narcissism) you can communicate to them in a way that appeals to the seemingly unpersuadable.	Part 3 Step 4: Busting barriers – Your audience unpersuadable personality traits
• The **SHIFT model** suggests ways of overcoming common communication barriers generated by *Social norms, unsustainable Habits; established Identities, strong negative Feelings towards sustainability; lack of Tangible advantages.*	Part 3 Step 4: Busting barriers – Common barriers to SHIFTing behaviours
• Your audience's perception of sustainability might be affected by a number of **cognitive biases**, from cognitive dissonance to negativity bias. Think about the potential objections you might get which can be dictated by those, from the obvious ones ("We don't have resources/time") to the ones	Part 3 Step 4: Busting barriers – Cognitive biases

that are specific to the topic you'll discuss or the type of person you are meeting.	
• Is there anything in your line of argument that could threaten the audience's *Status, Certainty, Autonomy,* or sense of *Relatedness and Fairness* **(SCARF)**? • How can you **pre-empt their objections**?	Part 1: The psychology of influencing: the predictably irrational way humans behave - – The SCARF model of social behaviour applied to business interactions
• Craft any relevant **case studies** that can support your point, inspire your audience and reassure them about their potential doubts or objections. • Showcase the challenges as well as the solutions for added interest and remember to highlight how sustainability is the magic potion and you are the wizard that supports others to become the heroes of the story. • Use proven **storytelling techniques**, like *And, But, Therefore,* to add interest to case studies.	Part 1: The psychology of influencing: the predictably irrational way humans behave – The SCARF model of social behaviour applied to business interactions Part 2: How to shift mindsets to communicate sustainability successfully – How can I influence other people's behaviour? – How does communication change from conversations to presentations? Step 2: Goals Project vs. strategic sustainability goals: how to persuade your audience to go for more – Hone the art of persuasion Step 4: Busting barriers – Storytelling

During the meeting or presentation	Chapter
• **Be present. Listen. Ask open and deep questions.** Once you know more about who you are meeting, you can ask specific questions about them that will open up the conversation and start building quick rapport. • You can **map the stakeholders** before or after the first interaction, depending on how much information you have beforehand about the topic to be discussed and the people involved. Identify who you need to focus your efforts on, in particular *promoters*, especially if they sit at the boardroom table (who will have the interest and power to champion the sustainability cause with their powerful but less interested peers), and *defenders*, who can help you create a grassroots movement. • Don't forget to take into consideration **Nature as a silent stakeholder** at the decision table.	**Part 3:** **Step 1: Build rapport and explore the status quo**
• Remember not to start the interaction as the expert with all the solutions: to co-create the perfect bespoke solution to any issue you'll need your audience's knowledge of their own company and sector, coupled with your sustainability expertise. • To establish the right goals for the conversation (and wider project), you'll need to **separate the audience's *needs* from their *wants*.** Asking about their *challenges* and adopting a "systems thinking" approach will uncover the root causes of the issue you want to address with your audience: their *needs*.	**Part 3:** **Step 2: Goals**

• If they have a specific idea about what they *want*, ask them how they reached this conclusion. This will highlight any discrepancies between wants and needs. • Don't forget to take into consideration **your own and Nature's goals**. • If your audience lacks ambition in their goals, or are nervous about embracing sustainability fully, adopt Greek philosopher **Aristotle's persuasion model:** *Ethos*: be credible and transparent; share examples of success stories; *Logos*: share data and details to support your arguments, address the doubts and demonstrate the advantages of sustainability; *Pathos*: aim at provoking emotions via your case studies, by making them more compelling and injecting some humour or other elements of interest in your presentation. • **Start small** if you really can't shift them towards more strategic sustainability goals: starting from a pilot project (*an anchor*) will help lower the barriers of resistance with the idea to adopt a more encompassing sustainability perspective in the future. • Consider what *support* you can offer your audience during the transition to a more sustainable way of doing business.	
• **Embrace co-creation**, which goes beyond simple collaboration by actively engaging all relevant stakeholders in your sustainability efforts so that collective intelligence is generated, and everyone's input is considered including the silent stakeholder' Nature.	**Part 3:** **Step 3: Co-creation**

• Openly **invite people to co-create** and explain how co-creation goes beyond mere collaboration. • Establish clear communication systems and ground rules. • Use the **"Yes... and" technique** to generate a flow of innovative ideas while ensuring that everyone feels heard and valued. • Embrace **systems thinking** by using tools like *causal loop diagrams* to visualize and understand the complex interconnections within sustainability challenges. By mapping out these systems, you can co-create comprehensive solutions that address root causes rather than just symptoms. • Plan on how to tackle the solutions step by step to avoid overwhelm starting with the end in mind to ensure you reach the set goals. • **Prioritize the actions that take the audience to the end goal faster, as opposed to short term fixes,** using the **multi-criteria prioritization table** (based on weighted criteria and what to *Continue, Stop, Reduce, Improve, Upskill on, Start or Innovate*). • Encourage the audience to use **feedback loops** to continuously learn and adjust the strategies used: sustainability is a fast-evolving science and needs a flexible approach.	
• A major barrier can be **your own communication style:** you might have learned to overcomplicate things to demonstrate that you are knowledgeable, with the result of alienating people.	**Part 3:** **Step 4: Busting Barriers**[127]

---

[127] As you are co-creating solutions, some barriers are bound to come up from your audience. Since these are best looked up *before* your conversations, I have already summarized them in the table: "Before the meeting or presentation".

• Be an *active listener*. Pay attention to the speaker's verbal and nonverbal cues, ask clarifying questions, and summarize what you've heard to ensure understanding. • Mind your *body language*: Make eye contact, project an open posture, and avoid fidgeting. These nonverbal cues signal that you're engaged and interested in the conversation. • *Tailor your message* to your audience: consider your listener's background, knowledge level, and interests. Use clear, concise language and avoid jargon or overly technical terms. • *Practise empathy*: Try to see things from the other person's perspective. This will help you understand their needs and tailor your communication accordingly.	
• The final step in this process focuses on securing **your audience's commitment** to sustainability and encouraging **continuous improvement.** • When there is nervousness around sustainability, by proposing to commit to a modest initial step, an *anchor,* you can demonstrate the feasibility of the change and lower any resistance. • This *anchor* should be clearly defined, measurable, and widely communicated across the entire company. This transparency fosters accountability and allows everyone to track progress. • Ensure any *commitment aligns with the company's core values*. Values act as a compass, guiding behaviour and decision-making. If there's a misalignment between the proposed sustainability practices and the company's existing values, gaining buy-in will be difficult and lasting change improbable.	**Part 3:** **Step 5: Commitment and way forward**

• *Leadership needs to be on board* for this initiative to succeed. Remember, as discussed in Step 4, even seemingly resistant leaders can be persuaded with persistence and strategic focus. • Encourage your audience to *review regularly their goals, commitments and progress* to keep on track.	

Appendix B: Systems thinking: what it is and why it's helpful in sustainability

We live in a VUCA (Volatile, Uncertain, Complex and Ambiguous) world. In sustainability, the complex causal interconnections between elements make it harder to predict the future. Overpopulation, biodiversity loss, pollution, man-made substances that the Earth ecosystems cannot re-absorb and climate change are all complex issues with a myriad of causes and consequences, all interconnected with each other. A simple cause-and-effect model is not sufficient to find solutions to the complex problems we face.

As human beings, we are used to a reductionistic and dualistic way of looking at problems: for problem A there is solution B. For instance, if we want to reduce plastic pollution, we think we can package our drinks in recycled plastic bottles.

The problem is that a simple solution of this kind doesn't take into consideration how much energy goes into repurposing recycled plastic; that plastic is actually very difficult to recycle,[128] that currently less than 10% of plastic is recycled worldwide[129] and so on.

---

[128] Greenpeace USA. (2022, October 26). *Circular claims fall flat again* | Greenpeace USA. www.greenpeace.org/usa/reports/circular-claims-fall-flat-again/
[129] Ritchie, H., Samborska, V., and Roser, M. (2023, December 28). *Plastic pollution. Our World in Data.* https://ourworldindata.org/plastic-pollution

This is where systems thinking comes, as an invaluable approach to addressing complex issues.

But what is a *system?*

Donella Meadows (2009, *Thinking in Systems*) wrote:

> A system isn't just any old collection of things. A system is an interconnected set of elements that is coherently organised in a way that achieves something. If you look at that definition closely for a minute, you can see that a system must consist of three kinds of things: *elements, interconnections,* and a *function* or purpose.

As an example, a tree is a system composed of *elements* such as roots, trunk, branches, leaves and flowers. Its *interconnections* include the flow of nutrients and water through the roots and trunk, the process of photosynthesis in the leaves, the transport of sugars through the phloem, and the interactions with pollinators and the surrounding ecosystem. The *purpose* of the tree can be to grow and reproduce, provide habitat for various species, contribute to the oxygen and carbon cycles, or enhance the beauty and health of its environment.

Likewise, our bodies are systems (with sub-systems in them like the cardiovascular, respiratory, or lymphatic system), and so are cities, football teams, schools.

In reality, systems are human constructions that help us make sense of our complex world. Ultimately, everything is made of atoms and molecules and under a microscope we are made of the same stuff of rocks and the ocean.

For this reason, when thinking in systems, it is helpful to understand or establish their *boundaries*: in the tree example, the boundaries of the system can be the tree itself, from its leaves to its roots.

Another important aspect of systems is that they change their behaviour *over time*, mostly in a non-linear way. They might show some repeating *patterns* (trees blossom in spring, then shed leaves in autumn), but we might not know exactly when they occur since their behaviour is affected by *interconnected elements* (e.g., the weather, the location, the soil and so on).

In order to understand and attempt to predict the behaviour of a system, systems thinkers strive to:

- see the whole picture, as opposed to the single elements

- look for interdependencies between elements

- take a wider perspective, and consider multiple points of view

- consider how mental models create our future and challenge them

- look at the system's evolution over time, especially long-term

- look for the root causes and improvements, and

- make systems visible through *causal maps* and *models*, like the Iceberg Model (see the next section).

When supporting clients to address their sustainability issues, or when you are facing issues of your own, it's always helpful to use a systems thinking perspective. In sustainability, nothing is straightforward and although systems thinking does not guarantee a perfect solution every time, it helps spot risks and opportunities, and develop solutions that are fit for purpose for the longer term.

The Iceberg Model

The Iceberg Model is a valuable tool for fostering systemic thinking, because it encourages linking an event – a single incident or occurrence – to patterns of behaviour, system structures, and mental models. This approach reveals the hidden structures underlying the event, much like an iceberg, where 90% of its mass is submerged and invisible.

By identifying and connecting these hidden structures to the events we observe, we can develop lasting solutions that address the entire system, rather than short-term, reactive solutions.

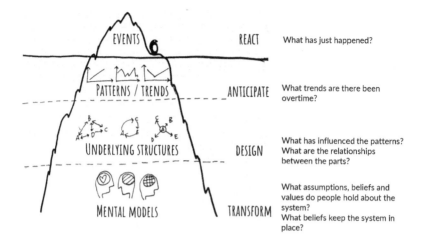

Figure 17 *How to think in systems*

In Step 2 we have used the example of a supermarket chain wanting to acquire a new electric fleet of vehicles for their deliveries.

Let's use the Iceberg Model to work out whether this particular solution is the right one for this client, taking into consideration the wider context.

We are going to ask some questions going from "the tip of the iceberg", which is the fact we are analysing, progressively down to the bottom, to understand the mental models and structures that the directors of this supermarket chain have, which led to this conclusion:

1. What trends and patterns have led to this point?

Trends: the world is accelerating towards electrification of vehicles. Marketing is pushing EVs left right and centre. The commercial electric vehicles market is lit up with a 35% year-on-year increase in sales.[130] Some obvious issues are still limiting its full uptake: price tags, battery disposal, relatively limited mileage range and an electric infrastructure with growing pains that is still not adequate to the booming demand.

---

[130] Trends in electric cars – Global EV Outlook 2024 – Analysis – International Energy Agency (2024). www.iea.org/reports/global-ev-outlook-2024/trends-in-electric-cars

Patterns: since 2015, the EV market has been growing exponentially, led by Nissan, which made its Leaf a utilitarian electric dream, and by Tesla, the Apple of the EV market, which set a trend and made EVs a status symbol. The leap from private vehicles to commercial is happening, with the global commercial vehicle market projected to increase by 25% by 2030.[131]

2. What has influenced these patterns and trends? What are the relationships between the parts?

Influencing factors: there are a number of factors that have influenced this decision: from some obvious economic and environmental advantages (lower maintenance, lower running costs, lower air pollution where the vehicle is operated) to some drivers, like the regulatory pressure to reduce vehicle emissions, grants and fast improving technology to the opportunity to enhance their reputation in front of their customers. But there is also an element of comparison with businesses who have already jumped on the trend and have electrified their fleets.

Relationship between the parts:

- The vehicle fleet the client wants will be part of a system of EVs, connected by a charging infrastructure that will support it.

- The charging infrastructure uses electricity from both renewable and fossil fuels, in different percentages depending on the country, time of year and day. The fact that the fuel will not always be zero emissions (unless the client has installed onsite renewable energy sources that will power the vehicles) can be an issue when considering Scope 3 emissions.

- The vehicles will be made of parts, which will require virgin resources, including metals and compounds such as cobalt, lithium and nickel. These resources rely on supply chains that employ people in different parts of the world, in areas in which it is hard to verify ethical labour practices and fair pay.

---

[131] Electric Commercial Vehicle Market Insights | Electric Commercial Vehicle Market Size & Share Analysis – Growth Trends & Forecasts (2024–2029). www.mordorintelligence.com/industry-reports/electric-commercial-vehicle-market

- The old vehicles will be decommissioned and end up as waste or will need to be sold, an additional task for someone within the company.

- The costs of the new EVs will need to counterbalance the savings in fuel and maintenance.

- The logistics of the deliveries will need to change as the EVs will need more frequent charges. This implies additional training for the drivers.

3. What beliefs, assumptions and values do people hold about the system?

Because human beings tend to simplify to make sense of the complex systems around them, there is a tendency to over-simplify for the sake of quickly understanding and addressing an issue. There is a belief that EVs are *the only* way forward to show to the world that a business is sustainable. EVs are a quick get-out-of-jail-free card to be seen as a sustainable business by customers even if the numbers do not add up, there are concerns around labour practice or how to take into account Scope 3 emissions.

Another assumption could be that EVs are the only solution available to the client to reduce their transport-related emissions.

So, is the idea of changing all their commercial vehicle fleet the right solution for this client right now?

It depends.

This client might be unaware of the spread of potential solutions available to them, from delivery schedule adjustments, to smaller vehicles, to some second hand EVs as opposed to a whole new fleet, to driving techniques to save fuel.

Whether any of these are a valid alternative to your client's idea depends on:

- their current emission baseline

- their target emissions and deadline for achieving them

- their capital availability, potential government incentives and other financial implications

- the level of top management commitment and whether sustainability is part of their business strategy or not

- the implications of this decision on staff and the local community.

Appendix C: The business case for sustainability

When building up the business case for sustainability, there are plenty of advantages that you can present to your audience, which have been demonstrated in numerous studies across sectors. A brief online search should provide specific statistics, sources and references to back up your claims in your specific industry and country.

But as a starting point, here are the main value-creation levers of adopting sustainability split into three main categories:[132]

---

[132] Here are some references you can use as a starting point to build your business case for sustainability:

The business of sustainability (2011, October 1). McKinsey & Company. www.mckinsey.com/capabilities/sustainability/our-insights/the-business-of-sustainability-mckinsey-global-survey-results

Whelan, T. (2017, June 1). The Comprehensive Business Case for Sustainability. *Harvard Business Review.* https://hbr.org/2016/10/the-comprehensive-business-case-for-sustainability

Ditlev-Simonsen, C. D. (2022). A Guide to Sustainable Corporate Responsibility. From Theory to Action.

Goodbody Clearstream (2023, April 11). *The business case for sustainability* [Video]. YouTube. www.youtube.com/watch?v=LKf3mxi0YMY

Harding, G. (2023, August 21). *The business case for sustainability.* Cambridge Institute for Sustainability Leadership (CISL). www.cisl.cam.ac.uk/news/blog/business-case-sustainability

Return on Investment	Risk Management	Growth
Cost and operational savings	Avoiding fines/law compliance	Talent attraction and retention
Higher rental/sales yields	Due diligence	Customer attraction and retention
Quicker sales	Operational risk management	Advantage over competition
Access to finance	Good governance[133]	Innovation and quality
Increased staff and operational productivity	Resilience	
	Enhanced brand and reputation	
	Licence to operate	
	ESG/CSR policy compliance	

Why 2024 is the year sustainability develops a business case (2024, September 10). World Economic Forum. www.weforum.org/agenda/2024/01/why-2024-is-the-year-of-the-business-case-for-sustainability-davos/

The business case for sustainability (2024). Deloitte United States. www2.deloitte.com/us/en/pages/consulting/articles/the-business-case-for-sustainability.html

[133] *Good Governance*, as outlined in ISO 37000: 2021, revolves around a set of principles and practices designed to ensure that organizations are directed, controlled, and held to account in a transparent, ethical, and effective manner. The key elements of good governance are Accountability, Transparency, Ethical Conduct, Sustainability, Stakeholder Engagement, Strategic Direction, Performance Monitoring, Risk Management. By adhering to these principles, organizations can enhance their governance structures, leading to better decision-making, increased accountability, and overall improved organizational effectiveness and trust. ISO 37000 Governance of organizations – Guidance (n.d.). https://committee.iso.org/ISO_37000_Governance

Table of figures

Index

Page numbers in *italics* indicate tables, figures or highlighted text.

A quick word from Practical Inspiration Publishing...

We hope you found this book both practical and inspiring – that's what we aim for with every book we publish.

We publish titles on topics ranging from leadership, entrepreneurship, HR and marketing to self-development and wellbeing.

Find details of all our books at: www.practicalinspiration.com

 Did you know...

We can offer discounts on bulk sales of all our titles – ideal if you want to use them for training purposes, corporate giveaways or simply because you feel these ideas deserve to be shared with your network.

We can even produce bespoke versions of our books, for example with your organization's logo and/or a tailored foreword.

To discuss further, contact us on info@practicalinspiration.com.

 Got an idea for a business book?

We may be able to help. Find out more about publishing in partnership with us at: bit.ly/PIpublishing.

Follow us on social media...

 @PIPTalking

@pip_talking

@practicalinspiration

@piptalking

Practical Inspiration Publishing